Sustaining High Performance in Business

Sustaining High Performance in Business

Systems, Resources, and Stakeholders

Jeffrey S. Harrison

BUSINESS EXPERT PRESS

Sustaining High Performance in Business: Systems, Resources, and Stakeholders
Copyright © Business Expert Press, LLC, 2020.

First published in 2020 by
Business Expert Press, LLC
222 East 46th Street, New York, NY 10017
www.businessexpertpress.com

ISBN-13: 978-1-95152-776-1 (paperback)
ISBN-13: 978-1-95152-777-8 (e-book)

Business Expert Press Strategic Management Collection

Collection ISSN: 2150-9611 (print)
Collection ISSN: 2150-9646 (electronic)

Cover image licensed by Ingram Image, StockPhotoSecrets.com
Cover and interior design by S4Carlisle Publishing Services Private Ltd., Chennai, India

First edition: 2020

10 9 8 7 6 5 4 3 2 1

Printed in the United States of America.

Abstract

Many books and articles have been written about how firms can achieve and sustain high performance. They typically focus on a particular aspect of the firm, such as its culture, resources, leadership, ability to learn, human resource practices, or communication systems. Often the very firms that are used as examples of high performance are no longer high performers even a few years later. In contrast, this book asserts that it is the efficiency and effectiveness of a firm's entire value creating system that determines its performance over the long term. Systems theory is used as an integrative mechanism to combine the best ideas from industrial organization economics, the resource-based perspective, and stakeholder theory. On the basis of this theoretical foundation, tools are provided for conducting in-depth, detailed analyses of each part of a firm's value creation system and its effectiveness in contributing to the total stakeholder value created by the firm. Systems assessment based on this information then leads to the development of strategies, including specific initiatives for overcoming weaknesses in the system and for creating new value for stakeholders. The book also provides guidance for developing detailed plans and a strategic control system to ensure strategies and initiatives are implemented. An underlying theme is that the purpose of a firm is to create value for its stakeholders: customers, employees, shareholders, suppliers, and the communities in which the firm operates. This book provides a concise yet complete guide for strategic management.

Keywords

strategic management; strategic planning; stakeholder management; stakeholder theory; systems theory; resource-based theory; resource-based perspective; business ethics; business strategy; corporate performance; corporate governance; corporate responsibility; sustainability; competitive advantage; sustainable competitive advantage; strategic control; strategy implementation

Contents

Contents

Introduction and Acknowledgments

The field of strategic management was in its infancy back in 1982, when I entered my doctoral program at the University of Utah. Like all business fields, strategic management was born out of necessity. Managers were looking for advice on how to help their firms navigate an increasingly volatile and complex business environment. Consultants and academics responded to the call, and one of the central questions we have continued to investigate is how to manage companies so that they will sustain a high level of economic performance. Many books have addressed this topic. In fact, it seems like every few years a book comes along that starts a *mini revolution* in business. Often these books are based on observations about *what the best firms do*. However, frequently the firms featured in these books lose their competitive edge just a few years later. For example, many business executives and scholars will remember that Jim Collins published a book called *Good to Great* that was intended to help organizations become great.[1] It sold over a million copies. However, a few years later, two scholars published a peer reviewed article in a highly regarded journal that demonstrated that of the 11 companies featured in Collins's book, only one continued to exhibit superior economic performance using the measure Collins used, and none of them were superior when an alternative measure was used.[2]

What if, instead of any one factor or feature, it is the entirety of an organization's value-creation system that determines its long-term economic performance? In other words, sustaining high performance is a function not only of the way each of the individual components of an organization is managed, but also of the way they are linked together. In this systems approach, the way the pieces and the whole system are connected to the external environment is critical. Although this perspective seems intuitive, and it is hard to refute, this is not the way most business books or articles are written, probably because making sense of such a complex, dynamic system would seem to be nearly impossible. This book, on the other hand, will help executives and students of strategic management adopt just such a perspective. It combines some of the tried-and-proven theories and methods from strategic management, stakeholder theory, and the resource-based perspective with systems theory in a practical way, such that readers will understand better what might be holding back an organization from even higher levels of performance and, once such performance is achieved, how to sustain it.

The material for this book comes from 35 years of research, consulting, writing, teaching, and numerous collaborations with some of the most influential business writers over the past several decades, including Ed Freeman, Bob Hoskisson, Mike Hitt, Duane Ireland, Jay Barney, Doug Bosse, Rob Phillips, Andy Wicks, and Tom Jones. I have learned a great deal from each of them. Some of this book also comes from *Foundations in Strategic Management*, 6th edition (2014). Caron St. John worked with me on the first four editions of that book, and I am indebted to her for her many contributions to it. I am also very grateful to Melody Bergman for carefully reviewing every aspect of this manuscript prior to submission. I am leaving out a lot of important people here in the interest of conciseness, but I simply must acknowledge the undeviating support I receive from my eternal partner, Marie, in all of my professional pursuits. This book is dedicated to her.

Notes

1. J. Collins. 2001. *Good to Great: Why Some Companies Make the Leap and Others Don't* (New York, NY: HarperCollins).
2. B.G. Resnick and T.L. Smunt. 2008. "From Good to Great to…," *Academy of Management Perspectives* 22, no. 4, pp. 6–12.

CHAPTER 1

A Systems Perspective on Strategic Management

The most successful organizations are able to acquire, develop, and manage valuable *resources and capabilities* that provide competitive advantages. Furthermore, they are capable of managing and satisfying a wide range of stakeholders. Resources and stakeholders, and the knowledge used to manage them, combine to make up the firm's *value creation system*. Top managers play a pivotal role in this process, as they help their companies interpret trends in the external environment, lead in the development of strategies, and oversee their execution. Strategic management involves the processes associated with managing the value creation system, including evaluating the competitive situation of a company, acquiring and managing resources and stakeholders, and developing and executing strategies.

The ultimate objective, or purpose, of the strategic management process is to help a firm create value for stakeholders, including customers, employees, suppliers, financiers (i.e., shareholders, creditors), and the communities in which the firm operates. Not long ago a statement like this would have been severely criticized by strategic management scholars as being illegal, impractical, or even immoral.[1] For several decades the received wisdom in business schools and among executives was that the purpose of a corporation is to maximize shareholder returns.[2] This logic extended to boards of directors, arguing that it is the fiduciary duty of directors to protect the interests of shareholders. Nonetheless, an obsession with shareholder returns carried with it a lot of unintended consequences, as executives made decisions that destroyed long-term value for their firms and for society. Huge scandals, such as the Enron debacle, began to shift public opinion against what is called *shareholder primacy* and toward a more balanced and responsible approach to management.

Over time, empirical evidence began mounting that addressing the interests of a broader group of stakeholders is associated with higher, not lower, economic performance.

Then, in 2019, the Business Roundtable, a group of CEOs from nearly 200 of the biggest corporations in the United States, released a signed statement defining the purpose of the corporation as serving employees, customers, suppliers, shareholders, and communities.[3] This signaled a major victory for stakeholder scholars, although those who have a vested interest in shareholder primacy undoubtedly will continue to argue against it.

Given the wide acknowledgment among business leaders that a firm has a broader purpose than simply maximizing financial returns, firm performance should also be measured more broadly—from multiple stakeholder perspectives. Table 1.1 contains some examples of performance measures for each of the five stakeholder groups specifically mentioned by the Business Roundtable. These measures are assessments of some of the value firms can provide to stakeholders, including but not limited to types of economic value. Many of these measures will be considered further in subsequent chapters in this book.

Table 1.1 Examples of firm performance measures from multiple stakeholder perspectives

	Value provided by firm	Potential measures
Employees	• Satisfaction with various components of employment contract (i.e., pay, benefits, perquisites) • Happiness with treatment (i.e., respect, honesty, inclusiveness, fairness) • Ability to develop and grow as individuals • Enjoyment from being part of a virtuous organization (organizational affiliation) • Enjoyment from providing value to customers	• Compensation and benefits • Workplace benefits (i.e., fitness center, childcare) • Legal actions or, if unionized, grievances • Productivity measures • Inclusion on list of best companies to work for • Internal promotions to top management • Turnover • Surveys of employee happiness with various aspects of the employment relationship

	Value provided by firm	Potential measures
Customers	• Satisfaction with product/ service features • Positive perception of value received to price paid for products/services • Happiness with treatment during transactions (i.e., respect, honesty, fairness) • Pride from associating with an organization with a positive social performance record	• Growth in sales • Consumer reports on products/ services • Reputation rankings • Surveys of customer satisfaction • Focus groups with customers • Existence or absence of customer-led legal actions
Suppliers	• Happiness with treatment during transactions (i.e., respect, honesty, fairness) • Payments on time and the right amount • Loyalty (consistent business dealings) • Sharing of information to improve operations	• Days payable outstanding (from accounting statements) • Longevity of supplier relationships • Existence or absence of supplier-led legal actions
Shareholders	• High financial returns • Low risk factors (consistency of returns) • Happiness with disclosure of pertinent information (transparency) • Satisfaction with firm's social performance • Happiness with firm's strategic direction and quality of management	• Shareholder returns • Return on shareholder equity (ROE) • Price-to-earnings ratio (P/E) • Risk associated with returns (i.e., variance and beta) • Number of shareholder proposals submitted (indication of shareholder unhappiness)
Community	• Happiness of community leaders and the general public with the overall impact of firm on the community and the environment • Community service programs • Philanthropy • Contributions to infrastructure (i.e., roads) • Employment of members of local community • Tax revenues	• Existence of community service programs • Percentage of income donated to community or other social causes • Tax breaks or other advantages provided to the firm (evidence of positive attitude toward the firm) • Existence or absence of community-led legal actions • Inclusion on list of socially responsible firms

The Strategic Management Process

Figure 1.1 illustrates the major activities of the strategic planning process and the major connections between them. The model is logical but is not intended to be rigid. These activities may be carried out in some other order or simultaneously. Note also the double headed arrows. They represent the idea that firms often cycle back to earlier activities of the strategic management process. For example, during the system assessment process, a firm may discover the need for more information, which will require more strategic analysis. Similarly, during implementation planning, managers may discover another problem area that requires attention, or they may actually need more information from either additional system assessment or more strategic analysis. Since more arrowheads would make Figure 1.1 difficult to read, the existing double arrow heads imply that a firm may need to revisit *any* of the other activities of the strategic planning process. And, of course, any of these activities may uncover the need to reexamine the strategic direction of the firm.

Strategic direction, examined in Chapter 3, encompasses the purposes of the firm, as manifest through its mission, vision, and values. It also includes a definition of its business model, including the markets it serves, its asset utilization strategy, the unique sources of value it provides to customers, and its basic growth strategy. Does the firm seek to manufacture the highest quality products or does it emphasize manufacturing a product that is adequate but at the lowest possible cost? Does the firm focus on a small customer segment or the whole market? Does the firm grow through internal development, acquisitions, or joint ventures? Answers to these questions provide a foundation upon which the firm's value creation system is managed. They provide direction to internal stakeholders as well as a strong signal to external stakeholders regarding what the firm is trying to do.

For most existing firms, strategic direction has already been established, even if it has not been formalized through written documents. However, at some point during the strategic planning process, it should be revisited, and preferably early, so that it can influence the rest of the process. Strategic analysis can help a firm determine if changes to strategic direction are required.

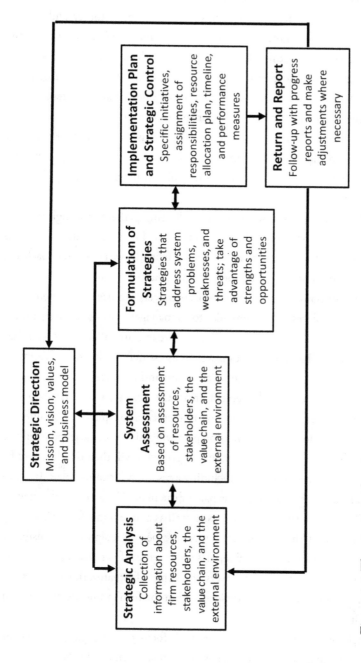

Figure 1.1 The strategic planning process

Strategic analysis, covered in Chapters 4 and 5, includes a variety of data collection activities that involve stakeholders inside and outside the firm. These activities include things like employee, customer, and supplier surveys and focus groups; internal financial analysis; competitor analysis; trend analysis; meetings with community leaders; and Internet searches. The idea is to collect enough information, called *strategic intelligence,* to give the firm a good idea regarding how its value creation system is functioning, on its own and in comparison to competitors; how well stakeholders are performing and their levels of satisfaction; and what are the changes in the external environment (i.e., industry, society, government, technology, economic) that are worthy of consideration during the planning process.

System assessment uses strategic intelligence gathered through the strategic analysis process to diagnose how well the value creation system is working and any areas that may be sufficiently weak to hold back the creation of more value in the system. Chapter 6 contains a variety of simple but powerful assessment tools managers can use to help determine these weak places. It also provides tools managers can use to determine if some areas in the system are receiving more resource allocations than they really need. The end result of a system assessment is the identification of problem areas that require more attention and resources.

Having determined problem areas, the next step is to develop specific initiatives as part of a formal implementation plan. As outlined in Chapter 7, a good implementation plan will assign specific responsibilities for each initiative to individual managers, who will then develop specific plans for carrying them out, including a resource allocation plan. In addition, a timeline is developed as part of the plan. Also, a control system is developed with specific objectives, as well as a time frame for their accomplishment. At the appropriate times, the person assigned responsibility for the initiative returns and reports on progress. If necessary, adjustments are made. Chapter 7 also covers the topic of organizational structure, which defines how work is divided within the firm's value creation system and its reporting structure.

Chapters 3 through 7 of this book focus on strategic planning for value creating systems at what is traditionally called the *business, business unit,* or *divisional* level. Each of these units has a top manager and a strategic direction. Some of the largest and most diversified corporations have dozens of business units, with managers of these units reporting to higher level managers. A business unit is defined in this book as a value creating system that could stand on its own, independent of the other business units of a diversified corporation, except perhaps that it would continue to acquire some of its resources from those other business units if it did separate from the firm. For diversified firms, then, there are value creation systems within a broader value creation system. Chapter 8 will apply systems thinking to the broader value creation system found in diversified firms. As opposed to the emphasis on the business level found in the first seven chapters, it will focus on what is called the *corporate* level and will include topics such as diversification strategy and synergy.

Strategic Thinking

This book will be more helpful if readers examine it from what, for many, will be a new way of thinking. Given the challenges of a complex and ever-changing business environment, what is needed is a comprehensive perspective on the firm that ties together all of the critical components of its system and fosters innovation. *Strategic thinking* is a term that is often used to describe the innovative aspects of strategic management, and it is perfectly aligned with a systems perspective.[4] The following characteristics are associated with the kind of thinking that is needed to stimulate innovation and a broad perspective in the strategic planning process.

1. *Systems Perspective.* Strategic thinking is systems thinking. The organization sits at the center of a network of stakeholders, and this network exists in the context of the sociocultural, economic, technological, and political/legal environment. Strategic thinking entails envisioning the whole value creation system, examining the actions a firm is taking or might take and analyzing how these actions are being influenced by or influencing that system. This approach helps in the generation of strategic alternatives, in their thoughtful evaluation, and in anticipating the reactions of external stakeholders, such as customers, competitors, or government regulators, to the actions a firm intends to take.

2. *Long-Term Oriented.* Some managers are so concerned about short-term operating details that they have a hard time focusing on where the firm is going. While it is true that efficiency often requires attention to details, it is also true that sometimes managers need to mentally step away from their day-to-day problems in order to focus on the future.

3. *Consideration of Past and Present.* Although strategic thinking is long-term oriented, it also includes learning from the past and recognizing the present. If organizations learn from the past, they can avoid making the same mistakes and can capitalize on the things they have done right. Managers also need to consider the constraints of the present. Some ideas that appear reasonable may fail because of lack of resources or poor timing.

4. *Intent Focused.* Some people think of creative processes as purely random and unstructured. However, strategic thinking is not a random process. It is based on a vision of where the organization is attempting to go. Strategic thinking leads to ideas that will help the organization achieve that vision.

5. *Ability to Seize Opportunities.* Managers sometimes encounter unanticipated opportunities that can further the intended strategies of the firm. The strategic planning process should be flexible enough to allow managers to take advantage of these opportunities when they occur.

6. *Hypothesis Testing.* The innovative ideas a firm generates about what it might do in the future are basically hypotheses. These hypotheses can and should be *tested* internally, on the basis of the information available, through rigorous analysis. However, it is important that a firm be willing to *pull the trigger* on ideas that make it through the analysis stage and actually try them. Often with new product introductions markets are tested in a limited geography. Also, new technologies may be applied only in particular areas of the firm. The firm then collects data to assess the success of the idea. If an idea is successful, it can be more broadly applied.[5]

Strategic thinking happens all the time, as employees and other stakeholders think of ideas that could be utilized in the firm. However, firms need to be positioned to take advantage of strategic thinking when it occurs.

There are several ways to foster strategic thinking.[6] First, organizations need to have systems in place to identify and evaluate good ideas when they occur. Some firms periodically allow employees to share ideas with top management. Even something as simple as an easily accessible online suggestion box can help with idea collection. Second, employees and other stakeholders must be encouraged to participate in strategic thinking and rewarded when they do. Rewards can include public recognition, money or other tangible gifts, promotions, a "thank you" from the CEO, a favorable contract extension, or many other things, depending on the stakeholder involved. Third, organizations should integrate the elements of strategic thinking directly into their strategic planning processes. For example, during a strategic planning meeting, participants might be asked to discuss ways to serve certain stakeholders better or respond to a societal change or a looming competitive threat. Fourth, organizations may need to provide managers and employees with training, sometimes through consultants, on how to think strategically. Finally, and perhaps most importantly, organizations have to foster a risk-taking atmosphere, in part by not harshly penalizing failures when they occur. Ultimately, it is the responsibility of top managers to foster change and guard against blindly protecting the status quo.

A rigid strategic planning process can drive out strategic thinking. For example, some firms require their managers to establish and follow very detailed plans that do not allow for deviations. Other firms harshly penalize their managers for failure, so they are afraid to try new ideas. Effective strategic planning processes incorporate creative aspects associated with strategic thinking in addition to the more methodological elements associated with information collection, evaluation of alternative strategies, and implementation of those strategies once they are selected.

Tools for Sustaining High Performance

The next chapter provides the theoretical foundation upon which the rest of the book is based. The foundation is like a three-legged stool. The first leg is the economic theory upon which much of the field of strategic management rested in the early days of development, with an emphasis on practical tools that are still highly relevant. The second leg is one of the most influential theories in all of strategic management, the resource-based perspective, which views the firm as a collection of resources. On the basis of this theory, the primary responsibility of managers is to develop or acquire—and then manage—resources that will help build and sustain a competitive advantage. The third leg is stakeholder theory, which envisions the firm as a network of constituencies called stakeholders. According to stakeholder theory, firms that have excellent relationships with a broad group of stakeholders are likely to create more value. Systems theory is the top of the stool. It is the integrative theory that ties the other three theories together. The combination of these four theories creates a comprehensive and practical foundation for strategic planning in a highly complex and ever-changing business environment.

This book is intended to help managers and students of management better understand how firms can sustain high economic performance over time. It also provides a set of tools for diagnosing a firm's value creation system and for making adjustments to that system that will unlock even more value creation. It describes a strategic planning process that can be used in large or small firms in a variety of industries and situations. The process described herein is based on, and draws from, decades of consulting, research, writing, and learning from colleagues, clients, and students.

Notes

1. M. Friedman. 1970. "The Social Responsibility of a Business is to Increase Its Profits," *New York Times Magazine*, September 13, pp. 32-33.
2. L.A. Stout. 2012. *The Shareholder Value Myth: How Putting Shareholders First Harms Investors, Corporations, and the Public* (San Francisco, CA: Berrett-Koehler Publishers, Inc.).
3. J.S. Harrison, R.A. Phillips, and R.E. Freeman. 2019. "On the 2019 Business Roundtable 'Statement on the Purpose of a Corporation,'" *Journal of Management*. Doi: 10.1177/0149206319892669.
4. Y. Salamzadeh, V.Z. Bidaki, and T. Vahidi. 2018. "Strategic Thinking and Organizational Success: Perceptions from Management Graduates and Students," *Global Business and Management Research* 10, no. 4, pp. 1–19.

5. T. O'Shannassy. 2003. "Modern Strategic Management: Balancing Strategic Thinking and Strategic Planning for Internal and External Stakeholders," *Singapore Management Review* 25, pp. 53–67; J.M. Liedtka. 2001. "Strategy Formulation: The Roles of Conversation and Design." In *Handbook of Strategic Management*, eds. M.A. Hitt, R.E. Freeman, and J.S. Harrison (Oxford, UK: Blackwell Publishers), pp. 70–93; J.S. Harrison and C.H. St. John. 2014. *Foundations in Strategic Management.* 6th ed. (Mason, OH: South-Western).

6. B.-J. Moon. 2013. "Antecedents and Outcomes of Strategic Thinking," *Journal of Business Research* 66, pp. 1698–708; E.F. Goldman and A. Casey. 2010. "Building a Culture that Encourages Strategic Thinking," *Journal of Leadership & Organizational Studies* 17, no. 2, pp. 119–28.

CHAPTER 2

Alternative Perspectives on Strategy Development and Performance

The field of strategic management blends a wide variety of ideas representing many functional areas of business and an assortment of theoretical streams. The next several sections contain a brief explanation of some of the major theories and ideas upon which my model of the strategic management process is based, with systems theory as the integrative mechanism that ties them all together. Each of these major theoretical streams has its own ideas regarding what leads a firm to high economic performance.

Industrial Organization Economics

Early in the development of the field now called *strategic management*, a firm's external environment, and especially its industry, was considered the primary determinant of which strategies would likely be successful.[1] One of the early ideas that became popular during this time was *environmental determinism*, which suggests that good management is associated with determining which strategy will best fit environmental, technical, and human forces at a particular point in time and then working to carry it out.[2] From a deterministic perspective, the most successful organization will be the one that best *adapts* to existing forces. During this early period, competitive success was seen to be a function of devising and implementing strategies that take advantage of internal strengths (S) and overcome weaknesses (W), as well as taking advantage of environmental opportunities (O) and neutralizing external threats (T).[3] Sometimes called *SWOT analysis*, this tool is still used to summarize the results from internal firm and external environment analysis.

The field of *industrial organization economics*, which examines factors that lead some industries to be more profitable than others, provided ample theory upon which early strategic management scholars could draw. The industrial organization economics perspective is frequently referred to as the structure–conduct–performance model. The basic argument is that the economic performance of an industry is dependent on the conduct of the firms it contains, which is dependent on the structure of the industry.[4] *Structure* may be defined as factors that determine the competitiveness of the market, such as demand conditions, supply conditions, technology, and barriers to the entry of new firms.[5]

The industrial organization economics perspective has contributed significantly to the field of strategic management over the years, especially in understanding industry environments and how firms can deal with external forces. However, environmental determinism is no longer accepted as a primary guide for the formulation of strategies. After a critical review of environmental determinism, a well-known researcher argued as follows:

> There is a more fundamental conclusion to be drawn from the foregoing analysis: the strategy of a firm cannot be predicted, nor is it predestined; the strategic decisions made by managers cannot be assumed to be the product of deterministic forces in their environments . . . On the contrary, the very nature of the concept of strategy assumes a human agent who is able to take actions that attempt to distinguish one's firm from the competitors.[6]

Research supports the idea that while firm economic performance is determined, in part, by characteristics of the industries in which it participates, those characteristics are not the primary determinant of performance.[7] The notion of adaptation has been supplemented by the principle of *enactment*, which assumes that organizations do not have to submit to existing forces in the environment—they can, in part, shape their environment through strategic actions.[8] However, it is not necessary to completely reject determinism and the view that organizations should adapt to their environments or the more modern view that organizations can alter their environments through enactment. In reality, the best run organizations are engaged in the processes of adaptation and enactment simultaneously, influencing those parts of the environment over which the firm can exercise some control and adapting to environmental circumstances that are either uncontrollable or too costly to influence.

The Resource-Based View of the Firm

Another perspective on strategy development has gained wide acceptance since the 1980s, and it continues to be a core theory in the field. It is called the *resource-based view of the firm* and has its roots in the work of the earliest strategic management theorists.[9] According to this view, an organization is a bundle of resources that fall into the general categories of (1) financial resources, including all of the monetary resources from which a firm can draw; (2) physical resources, such as plants, equipment, locations, and access to raw materials; (3) human resources, which pertain to the skills, background, and training of individuals within the firm; (4) knowledge and learning resources, which help the firm to innovate and remain competitive; and (5) general organizational resources, which include a variety of factors that are peculiar to specific organizations. Examples of general organizational resources include the formal reporting structure, reputation, brands, management techniques, knowledge found in the organization and the systems that help to create it, organizational culture, and relationships within the organization, as well as relationships with external stakeholders.

According to the theory, if a resource that a firm possesses has value in allowing a firm to take advantage of opportunities or neutralize threats, if only a small number of firms possess it, if the organization is aware of the value of the resource and is taking advantage of it, and if it is difficult to imitate, either by direct imitation or substitution for another resource, then it may lead to a *sustainable competitive advantage*.[10] A sustainable competitive advantage is an advantage that is difficult to imitate by competitors and, thus, leads to a higher-than-average economic performance over a long time period. For example, Toyota has been able to create and maintain a high-performance knowledge-sharing network with its suppliers and other stakeholders, which has led to very high levels of efficiency and innovation.[11] Some strategy scholars believe that effective acquisition and development of organizational resources is the most important reason that some organizations are more successful than others.[12]

A tangent to the resource-based perspective focuses on *dynamic capabilities*.[13] It was developed to explain why firms are able to establish competitive advantage even amid rapid change. It stresses "exploiting existing internal and external firm-specific competences to address changing environments."[14] In the dynamic capabilities approach, *dynamic* refers to the ability of the firm to adapt to changes in the external environment and the word *capabilities* refers to strategic management skills that allow such adaptation.

Substantial research evidence exists to support the idea that the characteristics of the resources *and* capabilities firms possess influence their economic performance.[15] Nonetheless, although the criteria of resource value, rarity, and inimitability are useful knowledge, it is difficult to explain successful companies that do not seem to possess resources that satisfy all of the criteria. Furthermore, few resources are able to provide competitive advantage permanently or even for extended periods—the power of motivated imitation means that they will be copied, invented around, or otherwise compromised long before they have reached the end of a technological life cycle.

Also, the resource-based perspective provides limited guidance to managers with regard to which strategies a firm should pursue. Jay Barney, one of the most influential scholars on this topic, working with Asli Arikan, another business scholar, stated,

> It may often be the case that the link between a firm's resources and the strategies a firm should pursue will not be so obvious. For example, sometimes it might be the case that a firm's resources will be consistent with several different strategies, all with the ability to create the same level of competitive advantage. In this situation, how should a firm decide which of these several different strategies it should pursue?[16]

Consistent with this idea, a McKinsey survey of senior executives found 83 percent believe that shifting strategic resources such as money, talent, and management attention to where they are most needed is the best way to foster firm growth, but most are not sure where to reallocate it.[17]

A possible explanation for the existence of successful firms that do not seem to possess uniquely valuable and inimitable resources or capabilities is that the key to their success is found in the system that creates and utilizes firm resources and capabilities rather than in any one resource or capability itself. A pioneer of resource-based logic, Edith Penrose, wrote about the firm as follows:

> It is a complex institution, impinging on economic and social life in many directions, comprising numerous and diverse activities, making a large variety of significant decisions, influenced by miscellaneous and unpredictable human whims, yet generally directed in the light of human reason.[18]

We see in this description a complex system of humans engaged in a variety of economic and social activities. Consequently, there are threads in her resource-based work to both systems theory and stakeholder theory.

Stakeholder Theory

The stakeholder perspective of strategic management considers the organization from the perspective of the internal and external constituencies that have a strong interest in the activities and outcomes of an organization and upon whom the organization relies in order to achieve its own objectives. Jay Barney, whom we quoted previously as perhaps the foremost expert on the resource-based perspective, has said that a stakeholder perspective is necessary for resource-based theory to work.[19] His reasoning stems from the purpose of the corporation, which was discussed in Chapter 1. If the sole purpose of a firm is to generate high returns for shareholders, then the firm is going to have a very difficult time attracting the types of resources that are needed for the firm to be competitive. It is, after all, stakeholders that possess many of the resources needed for the firm's value creation system. For example, a firm that is heavily influenced by shareholder primacy may find it difficult to attract outstanding employees because wages and benefits are at a bare minimum. Similarly, if the firm is constantly cutting production costs so that shareholder returns are increased, at some point it will end up with a low-quality product that is not attractive to customers. Also, suppliers of the highest quality parts will probably find other firms more attractive because such a firm is likely to apply constant pressure on pricing.

Managing for Stakeholders

Many successful organizations have learned that taking especially good care of *primary stakeholders*, defined as those that are directly involved in the value creating processes of the firm, can lead to competitive advantages and high performance.[20] Some of these advantages, and the value they create, are outlined in Figure 2.1. This sort of management is often called *managing for stakeholders*. Managing for stakeholders implies that more attention and resources are allocated to satisfy the needs of stakeholders than might be necessary simply to retain their participation in the productive activities of the firm.[21] This also means that firms incur greater costs as, for example, they provide better wages and benefits to their employees, give back to the communities in which they operate, and provide high-quality products or outstanding service to customers at prices that are perhaps a little lower than they might otherwise charge.

Managing for stakeholders is economically feasible because it leads to behavior on the part of stakeholders that helps the firm create more value than might otherwise be created. Well-treated stakeholders *reciprocate* by treating the firm and its other stakeholders well in return. One of the fundamental drivers of this reciprocity is *fairness*, or what scholars call *organizational justice*.[22] Organizational justice can be broken into three primary types: distributional, procedural, and interactional.

Distributional justice means that stakeholders feel as though they are receiving value through their interactions with a firm that are commensurate with what they contribute to the firm. For example, an employee who gives extra effort to the firm feels as though they are compensated fairly for providing it. Compensation is not just economic, but includes noneconomic factors as well, such as other forms of recognition, positive feelings due to association with the firm, opportunities for personal development, and/or a feeling of job security.

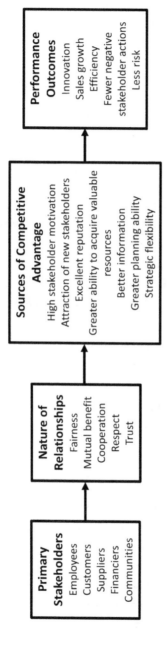

Figure 2.1 Strong stakeholder relationships leading to high value creation

Primary Stakeholders
Employees
Customers
Suppliers
Financiers
Communities

Nature of Relationships
Fairness
Mutual benefit
Cooperation
Respect
Trust

Sources of Competitive Advantage
High stakeholder motivation
Attraction of new stakeholders
Excellent reputation
Greater ability to acquire valuable resources
Better information
Greater planning ability
Strategic flexibility

Performance Outcomes
Innovation
Sales growth
Efficiency
Fewer negative stakeholder actions
Less risk

For a customer, the value received in return for the price paid for a product includes the features of the product and how well it satisfies or exceeds expectations. Additional value comes from positive feelings associated with buying from a firm that shares similar values or has a stellar reputation, as well as the after-the-sale service and follow-up from the firm. What a stakeholder values and how much weight is given to each factor is a function of what is called the stakeholder's *utility function*, and each stakeholder's utility function is a little different. However, firms can still do research with their stakeholders (i.e., surveys, focus groups, personal interviews) to determine some of the patterns among them with regard to what they value the most, and can then use this information during their strategic planning processes. The next few chapters provide guidance for how to do this.

Procedural justice means that the firm gives stakeholders voice and considers their positions when making important decisions that are likely to affect them. This does not mean that the firm will always make decisions that have no negative impact on any stakeholder, although this is a worthwhile objective. It does mean that stakeholders feel respected and included and that they believe that the decision-making process was fair even if the outcome is not exactly what they most desired.

Procedural fairness comes with costs that are not as measurable as the costs associated with distributional justice, but have an impact nonetheless. Collecting and using information from a broad group of stakeholders takes time, which means that managers are diverting attention away from other responsibilities. An inclusive process can also slow down decisions. In addition, data management associated with this type of process requires dedicated resources, such as researcher assistance, a database, and technicians to manage it. Information has to be provided in the right form, at the right time, and to the right people for it to have a positive impact on decision making.

A final form of organizational justice is called *interactional justice*. It means that all stakeholders are treated with respect, integrity, and honesty. Promises, as well as both formal and informal contracts, are made and kept. Day-to-day transactions with stakeholders typically are positive, and if something goes wrong, the firm does its best to remedy the situation. This is probably the least expensive form of justice for the firm; however, pursuing it also implies that a firm will not take advantage of stakeholders even if they could do so. For example, a firm that practices interactional justice would not gouge a customer who is in desperate need of a product in high demand, even though the customer would be willing to pay much more than the normal price. Such a firm would not secretly pollute the environment in the communities in which it operates even if there is a low possibility of being caught. And these types of firms pay their bills on time even if they would be unlikely to lose a supplier if they pay their bills 2 months late. In other words, a firm that practices interactional justice is not opportunistic in its interactions with stakeholders, and this implies forgoing some economic gains in the interest of maintaining trusting and cooperative relationships with stakeholders.

Returning to the principle of reciprocity, which is integral to the concept of organizational justice, stakeholders are likely to reciprocate through a higher level of motivation to work with the firm and provide a level of effort and loyalty that they might not provide to another firm in the same industry. Because these sorts of firms tend to develop strong reputations for fairness, new stakeholders will want to be affiliated with them. Communities will welcome expansions, job applications will be higher, and customers will want to buy from and remain loyal to the firm. Suppliers will want to sell to the firm, which means the firm will have more attractive buying propositions and an opportunity to acquire superior resources and develop highly competitive capabilities. In general, stakeholders will be more cooperative with the firm and with each other in value creating activities.

Organizational justice also leads to higher levels of stakeholder trust, and this means stakeholders will be much more likely to share information about their utility functions—what they value. This sort of information can be used to innovate in both products and services and in the way they are made, delivered, and serviced. All of these factors, taken together, mean that firms will have a much greater ability to plan, and will enjoy *strategic flexibility*, which can be defined as the ability to make changes to accommodate volatility in external factors associated with their industries or their broader economic, societal, technological, or political/legal environments.[23]

These factors can lead to higher levels of innovation, sales growth, and operational efficiency. The contracting process is also more efficient, because high levels of trust mean that contracts will not need to contain as many safeguards or complicated contingency clauses.[24] In addition, because stakeholders are treated well and promises to them are kept, they are much less likely to pursue negative actions such as boycotts, legal suits, walkouts and strikes, lobbying for new regulations, or negative social media activities. This means that a firm that emphasizes organizational justice is a less risky proposition for all of the firm's stakeholders, including those that invest time, material resources, energy, or money in the firm. Also, an enhanced reputation means that potential new stakeholders, such as new customers, new suppliers, and new employees with excellent qualifications, will be attracted to the firm. This can give the firm an edge as it competes with other firms for the most outstanding stakeholders.[25] These sorts of positive outcomes lead to a higher level of value creation than if a firm were to operate in a less fair and trustworthy fashion, especially if noneconomic factors are considered. However, from an economic perspective, the only way this sort of management pays off is if the economic benefits exceed the additional costs.

Contexts and Limits to a Stakeholder Approach

A significant amount of research evidence supports the view that firms that manage for stakeholders have higher economic performance in most contexts and industries.[26] Research is ongoing to identify situations in which more of an objective arms-length approach to managing stakeholders will produce better economic returns.[27] An *arms-length approach* means that transactions are strictly based on supply and demand market forces. Rather than developing close relationships with stakeholders, in which their interests are considered, the firm simply sees them as interchangeable suppliers or consumers of the factors of production. It is conceivable that such an approach could be more efficient in some rare instances in which innovation, loyalty, and higher levels of stakeholder motivation are not as important; however, it is doubtful researchers will ever find a context in a market economy in which consistently treating stakeholders unfairly and regularly violating their trust leads to increased long-term economic value. If we add in the negatives associated with lost stakeholder utility, then, the picture is likely to look even more bleak. Consider, for example, whether you would want to work for, invest in, provide supplies to, live next to, or buy from such a firm.

It is important to note that stakeholder theory does not suggest that firms should be overzealous in their relationships with stakeholders. Managers should exercise prudence when determining how much time, attention, and other resources to allocate to any particular stakeholder. Allocating too much value to stakeholders may result in a situation in which the firm is not able to sustain its core production or innovation processes.[28] One of the keys to managing for stakeholders is determining how much is too much when it comes to allocations to stakeholders. Chapter 5 provides tools to help accomplish the careful balancing act between too few and too many resources devoted to particular stakeholders.

To summarize, in strategic management, one of the first popular theoretical foundations for explaining high economic performance was provided by industrial organization economics, which suggested that industry is a dominant force in determining the performance of the firm. Eventually, we learned that industry is important, but not as important as other factors. Resource-based theory was also offered as a way to explain high economic performance that is sustainable over time. The resource-based perspective establishes criteria that help managers understand which resources are most valuable to competitive advantage, but does not explain how firms develop those resources or why some firms are competitive over long periods of time without possessing resources that satisfy all of the criteria. There is more to high performance than resource-based theory can explain on its own. Stakeholder theory suggests that high performance over time is a function of the way a firm manages relationships with its stakeholders, and the links between resources and stakeholders are strong—you can't have one without the other. What is needed is a way to tie together all three of these theories, and in a manner that provides guidance to managers to help them make strategic decisions. Systems theory achieves this objective.

Systems Theory[29]

In many industries multiple firms are pursuing what are essentially similar strategies with somewhat similar resources at their disposal, but with varying levels of performance success. Examples include package delivery, banking, and airlines. Performance variation in these cases is more a function of how firms develop, otherwise acquire, and utilize their resources than of the resources themselves. Connected to each resource are the stakeholders that actually provide or develop these resources and then utilize them to create value within the organization's system. As stakeholder theory experts Edward Freeman, Robert Phillips, and Rajendra Sisodia explain:

> In an interconnected and interdependent system, each stakeholder must be a means to an end. Each contributes to collective flourishing and each must also benefit for the system to continue flourishing. Every business is a system, embedded within a set of larger systems.[30]

One of the most important insights of systems theory as it applies to organizations is that *firms are open systems*, in that they are dependent on their external environments for survival.[31] They exchange information, materials, money, and energy with their external environments. This means that a firm's value creation system is inseparably connected to its external stakeholders. The open systems perspective is in contrast to viewing the organization as a closed system, meaning that the organization is closed off from external influences. The goal of a closed system is to make it as internally efficient as possible, while protecting it from any outside influences that could reduce efficiency. Obviously, such an assumption is ridiculous in an organizational setting.

Another important insight from systems theory is that a system is not understood as merely the sum of its parts.[32] Rather, it can only be understood in its entirety. Such a system is constantly in search of a state of *dynamic equilibrium* through continuous inflows of information, materials, and energy (with money as a facilitator of exchange), which are then transformed into outputs and exported into the external environment. The inflows and outflows are a reflection of the fact that the boundaries of an organization are permeable. Also, because the resources a firm acquires are *lumpy* (not infinitely divisible), adding resources in one area shifts the focus to another, requiring additional resources in one area after another.

This leads to productive growth, as the firm attempts to reach *an efficient balance of its resources—its equilibrium point.*[33]

A systems approach broadens the focus from bilateral transactions that are often implicitly assumed to scale up neatly to explain firm-level phenomena. Instead, it draws attention, from the beginning, to multi-lateral interdependencies among stakeholders, firms, and resources.[34] Furthermore, the diversity of individuals and subunits in organizations results in the presence of multiple objectives.[35] This is consistent with the move from an emphasis on serving shareholder interests to serving multiple stakeholders that was discussed in Chapter 1. Consequently, this book treats an organization's value creation system as a group of inter-related stakeholders and resources, dependent on the environment and organized to achieve multiple objectives. These objectives are viewed in stakeholder terms, where the ultimate objective is to create as much com-bined value for stakeholders as possible. As mentioned in the stakeholder section, there is empirical evidence that serving the interests of multiple stakeholders tends to be associated with high performance in traditional financial terms as well, so people who are still adamant about giving the highest priority to financial stakeholders, such as shareholders, can con-tinue reading in good conscience.

Interconnected Parts

Because a system is composed of interdependent parts, a change in one part of the system affects other parts, whether intentional or not. This idea is illustrated in Figure 2.2, which displays firm resources across five areas that are frequently discussed in the resource-based literature. In this figure, physical resources include the physical structures, systems, and equipment used to create products and services, directly or in support roles. General organization resources consist of a firm's reputation, as well as assets such as brands and patents. Knowledge and learning resources include the knowl-edge found in the organization and the systems used to collect, store, orga-nize, and disseminate this knowledge. They also include learning systems for creating new knowledge, such as research and development programs. The finance and human resource areas are self-explanatory. A firm can also develop capabilities in any one of these areas.

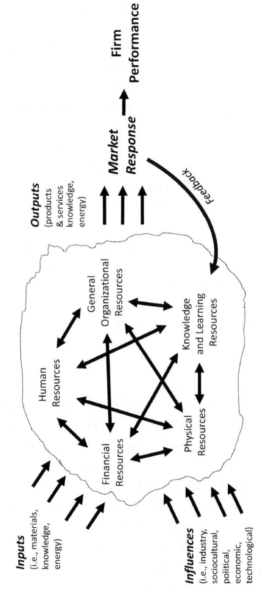

Figure 2.2 Organizational resource interconnectedness

The resources illustrated in Figure 2.2 are interdependent because resources in one area of the firm influence creation of resources in another area, which leads to another area, until the cycle eventually comes back to influencing resources in the original area.[36] The ability of a firm to produce attractive products and services is a function of the efficiency and effectiveness of the value creation system, where products and services are the result of managing the interdependent resources of the firm. The value creation cycle can work in positive or negative ways. That is, just as outstanding resources in one area can positively influence resources in another area, poor resources in one area can hurt the contributions of resources across the entire system. The interconnectedness of resources can be illustrated with a simple example. Financial resources are used to acquire the human resources needed to help the organization achieve its goals. If financial resources are weak, the firm will not be able to acquire high-level, talented, and hardworking employees. Subpar human resources are likely to impact knowledge and learning resources because the people hired are not as talented or creative. This will adversely impact the quality of products and services and, therefore, the reputation of the firm and its products and services (e.g., general organization resources). Demand drops, resulting in an inability to acquire the necessary financial resources to regenerate the system. This sort of logic holds regardless of where in the system the example begins.

Viewing resources in this way, it becomes apparent that the resource area that is the weakest, given the environment in which a firm competes (i.e., industry, economy), is the one that should be given the most managerial attention and resources. Based on systems theory, this principle is akin to what chemists call a "limiting reagent."[37] For instance, if one chemical in a chemical reaction gets used up before the other chemicals, then it is the one that is holding back the reaction from producing more of the product. Similarly, in biology, a nutrient that is in short supply relative to the others will limit cellular growth. Biologists call this a "limiting nutrient."[38] Both of these limiting factors are based on Liebig's Law of the Minimum, which states that growth is not constrained by the total sum of resources, but rather by the scarcest resource.[39] The concept of a limiting factor has also been applied to a variety of business situations across a fairly substantial time frame, such as the growth of chain stores, product manufacturing, and information technology innovation.[40]

From a systems perspective, the goal of any one part of the system is to make the whole system better.[41] A limit in one resource area can negatively influence firm efficiency and, thus, the growth of resources and competitive advantage in the entire value creation system. Consequently, improving the resource position in the limiting resource area influences the ability of the firm to improve its resource position in all of the major resource areas, which leads to more attractive products and services, resulting in competitive advantage and higher firm performance.

Although it may be one area of the value creation system that requires intensive effort and attention, other areas should not be simultaneously neglected. In other words, organizational changes should be planned systematically, rather than focusing on one organizational segment. A systems expert stated this well:

> Most managers have an implicit mental model which says that change efforts are additive. In other words, if managers generate enough change initiatives, and fast enough, they'll be successful in large-scale organizational change. Nothing could be further from the truth. As systems, organizations have components that interact—much like multiple drugs have interactions within the human body.[42]

Permeable Firm Boundaries

The dotted line surrounding the inner core of the value creation system in Figure 2.2 reflects the principle that firms, as open systems, have permeable boundaries, which means that boundaries between a firm's internal and external environments are blurry and interactions across those boundaries are viewed as parts of ongoing, often collaborative, processes rather than as a series of finite transactions.[43] Firms rely on their external environments to acquire resources and are dependent on their external environments for survival.

As illustrated in Figure 2.3, a firm is dependent on various external stakeholders that possess tangible and intangible resources the firm needs for its value creation system to function effectively. For example, recruiting new employees depends on the availability of external labor pools just as securing financing depends on sales to customers and relationships with banks and other financiers. As discussed in the stakeholder section, firms that have strong, mutually beneficial and trusting relationships with their stakeholders are in a better position to obtain resources that will lead to competitive advantage. For instance, a firm with a reputation for treating stakeholders well is more attractive to stakeholders such as customers and suppliers, which means that they are more likely to buy the firm's products or enter into contractual agreements with them. Consequently, firms can improve their value creation system and, thus, stimulate performance by improving their relationships with the stakeholders that are linked to resource areas in which the firm is currently weak.

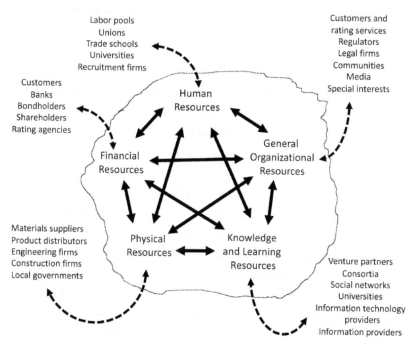

Figure 2.3 Examples of stakeholders connected to resources

Dynamic Equilibrium

In the introduction to this section, dynamic equilibrium was described as a state in which all components of a system are in balance—when adding more of one particular component will not create more output. Applied to a firm's value creation system, this would mean that improving or adding more of a particular resource will not lead to more value for stakeholders or to a higher performance. Of course, this is impossible from a practical perspective. Even if a state of dynamic equilibrium were achievable, as systems theory suggests, it is not likely to last, precisely because firm resources and the environments upon which they depend are constantly changing. At the firm level, many resources wear out, people leave, relationships change, and new knowledge is created on a regular basis. In the external environment, new technologies, sociocultural trends, economic changes, and political forces all work to put a firm's system in a state of disequilibrium. Consequently, seeking a state of equilibrium is a desirable objective rather than a likely outcome—it unleashes the creation of more value even if the total amount of value is never really maximized.

The concept of dynamic equilibrium introduces a temporal dimension. Related to stakeholders, it may not be reasonable to expect *immediate* increases in financial resources when firms begin to work on improving relationships with the stakeholders associated with a particular resource area. In fact, the opposite may be the case because improvements can cost more in the short term than they return in immediate resource increases, much like an investment in research and development. However, just like R&D, investments now can provide a much stronger future. As a simple example, assume a firm ships a product to a customer that satisfies the requirements of a contract but contains a defect that will cause it to wear out sooner than anticipated. As soon as the defect is noticed, managers contact the customer and replace the product with another one that is not defective. This is costly, but it builds a trusting relationship with the customer that is likely to pay dividends for many years in terms of new contracts and enhancing the firm's reputation.

In another example, a firm has many single mothers working for it, so it establishes a daycare facility on site that employees can use for their dependents. It is priced *at cost* or perhaps even a little below the cost to the firm, so it is a good deal for the employees. The benefits from employee reciprocity are obvious, but consider also that the firm is now much more attractive as an employer, which means it has a greater selection of the best qualified applicants. Returning to our value creation system, these better, more highly skilled employees create higher quality, innovative products more efficiently. Customer demand increases. Reputation is enhanced. In this case, some of the financial benefits will be immediate due to increased motivation and lower turnover, but some of them may take a while to materialize.

But what about the constant changes to resources and the environment? If fostering strong relationships with stakeholders is a long-term proposition, how can firms cope with these changes now? A firm with strong, mutually beneficial relationships with stakeholders is going to be more, not less, likely to be able to cope with changes. Returning to the three primary types of organizational justice discussed previously in this chapter (distributional, procedural, interactional), stakeholders that are treated with fairness are strong allies for firms that need to adjust to changing conditions. The upshot is that stakeholders who receive or anticipate fair treatment are more willing to share valuable information (i.e., not easily available to outside parties) about what they see happening in the external environment, as well as about their own underlying interests and capabilities and the interests and capabilities of other stakeholder groups with which they are acquainted.[44] A firm that genuinely understands the interests of its customers will be more effective in manufacturing products they find attractive. In addition, behavior that supports open dialogue about major and minor changes in roles, inputs, or outputs promotes collective commitments to the new courses of action.

By taking the time to include a firm's primary stakeholders in decisions about how they will work together, managers allocate procedural justice and provide important interactions through which they can learn about what their stakeholders expect. This knowledge helps calibrate exactly what needs to be done to meet or exceed stakeholder expectations and, thus, to trigger positive reciprocity and greater effort.[45] Positive reciprocity and greater effort from stakeholders can help the firm begin to experience improvements in weak resource areas within their value creation systems. The firm experiences improvements via bilateral posi-tive reciprocity as stakeholders recognize and appreciate that they have the ability to influence the firm and as they are motivated to provide valuable information and other resources to the firm with the expectation that some portion of the value cocreated with the firm will be distributed back to them in some form.

Learning from Feedback

Another systems concept suggests that open systems learn from feedback (note the feedback arrow in Figure 2.2). Of course, organizational learn-ing in response to external changes is also at the heart of the dynamic capabilities perspective.[46] However, the value creation system perspective used herein is more comprehensive, in that it examines the firm's whole system rather than a particular capability. This whole system includes the environment, as managers play a crucial role in interpreting a firm's envi-ronment so that the firm can make strategic changes in a timely fashion.[47] As such, managers can envision their firms as information networks, with the flow of information providing decision makers throughout the value creation system with information they need to make good decisions. Procedural justice, mentioned earlier in this chapter, typically involves giving stakeholders the chance to influence decisions that will affect their interests. Consequently, the comprehensiveness of a firm's information system can enhance performance.

Just like other long-term investments, the cost of building comprehen-sive information systems can reduce firm profitability in the short term. Nonetheless, firms with the best information systems are able to make the most effective use of external stakeholder resources in their value cre-ation systems and, thus, enjoy superior performance in rapidly changing environments. In other words, the quality and efficiency of a firm's infor-mation systems are likely to be an important variable in explaining the effectiveness of a firm's value creation system and its pattern of growth.

The Value Creation System

The emphasis in this book is on value creation systems, which comprises resources, stakeholders, and the external environmental influences to which they are subject. Unlike a traditional resource-based perspective, the systems emphasis is on how resources and capabilities are combined and created as opposed to focusing on the characteristics of particular resources. This perspective shares with the dynamic capabilities approach a common focus on the production of attractive end products as the ultimate avenue to market success and an emphasis on *organizational* change as a means to sustained success. However, unlike the dynamic capabilities approach, a firm is assumed to be able to increase its competitiveness through improving its ordinary capabilities as well as its dynamic capabilities. These ordinary capabilities include routine administrative, operating, and governance functions.[48] Also, the dynamic capabilities approach focuses on creating new resources and capabilities and not on coordinating their application. Dynamic capabilities are considered herein as subsystems of a larger system of value creation.

Stakeholders, such as employees, customers, suppliers, financiers, and the communities in which firms operate, hold the keys to resource acquisition, development, and utilization. They create the actual products and services that are disseminated into the market. They determine product and service quality. They determine how efficient the firm will be and how innovative. Therefore, the nature of the relationships a firm has with its stakeholders, both internal and external, has a large effect on its competitive success and economic performance. However, the context—the external environment—is also important. Consequently, the value creation system approach also embraces the practical side of industrial organization economics.

The strategic management process model upon which this book is based relies, to a great extent, on each of the theories and ideas that have been described in this chapter. They provide complementary rather than competing perspectives. Building on this foundation, Chapters 3 and 4 will provide a set of tools for collecting information about a firm's value creation system that will allow managers to make better decisions about where to allocate time and other resources.

Notes

1. N. Argyres and A.M. McGahan. 2002. "An Interview with Michael Porter," *Academy of Management Executive* 16, no. 2, pp. 43–52.

2. J. Bourgeois, III. 1984. "Strategic Management and Determinism," *Academy of Management Review* 9, pp. 586–96.

3. H.I. Ansoff. 1965. *Corporate Strategy* (New York, NY: McGraw-Hill); C. Hofer and D. Schendel. 1978. *Strategy Formulation: Analytical Concepts* (St. Paul, MN: West Publishing).

4. J.S. Bain. 1956. *Barriers to New Competition* (Cambridge, MA: Harvard University Press).

5. D.W. Carlton and J.M. Perloff. 2005. *Modern Industrial Organization*. 4th ed. (Upper Saddle River, NJ: Prentice Hall).

6. Bourgeois, "Strategic Management and Determinism," p. 589.

7. Y.-M. Chen and F.-J. Lin. 2010. "The Persistence of Superior Performance at Industry and Firm Levels: Evidence from the IT Industry in Taiwan," *Industry & Innovation* 17, pp. 469–86; J.C. Short, D.J. Ketchen, Jr., T.B. Palmer, and G.T.M. Hult. 2007. "Firm, Strategic Group, and Industry Influences on Performance," *Strategic Management Journal* 28, pp. 147–67.

8. L. Smirchich and C. Stubbart. 1985. "Strategic Management in an Enacted World," *Academy of Management Review* 10, pp. 724–36.

9. E.T. Penrose. 1959. *The Theory of the Growth of the Firm* (New York, NY: Wiley); B. Wernerfelt. 1984. "A Resource-based View of the Firm," *Strategic Management Journal* 5, pp. 171–80.

10. J.B. Barney. 1991. "Firm Resources and Sustained Competitive Advantage," *Journal of Management* 17, pp. 99–120. Wernerfelt, "A Resource-Based View."

11. J.K. Dyer and K. Nobeoka. 2000. "Creating and Managing a High-Performance Knowledge-Sharing Network: The Toyota Case," *Strategic Management Journal* 21, pp. 345–67.

12. M.J. Leblein. 2011. "What Do Resource- and Capability-Based Theories Propose?" *Journal of Management* 37, pp. 909–32.

13. D. Teece and G. Pisano. 1994. "The Dynamic Capabilities of Firms: An Introduction," *Industrial and Corporate Change* 18, pp. 509–33.

14. D. Teece, G. Pisano, and A. Shuen. 1997. "Dynamic Capabilities and Strategic Management," *Strategic Management Journal* 18, pp. 509–33.

15. T.R. Crook, D.J. Ketchen, Jr., J.G. Combs, and S.Y. Todd. 2008. "Strategic Resources and Performance: A Meta-analysis," *Strategic Management Journal* 29, pp. 1141–54. J.B. Barney and A.M. Arikan. 2001. "The Resource-Based View: Origins and Implications." In *Handbook of Strategic Management*, eds. M.A. Hitt, R.E. Freeman, and J.S. Harrison (Oxford, UK: Blackwell Publishers), pp. 124–88.

16. Barney and Arikan, "The Resource-Based View," 174.

17. Y. Atsmon. "How Nimble Resource Allocation Can Double Your Company's Value," *McKinsey & Company*. http://www.mckinsey.com/business-functions/

strategy-and-corporate-finance/our-insights/how-nimble-resource-alloca-tion-can-double-your-companys-value, (accessed January 3, 2017).

18. E. Penrose. 1959. *Theory of the Growth of the Firm* (Oxford, UK: Blackwell), p. 9.

19. J.B. Barney. 2018. "Why Resource-based Theory's Model of Profit Appro-priation Must Incorporate a Stakeholder Perspective," *Strategic Management Journal* 39, pp. 3305–25.

20. J.S. Harrison, W. Felps, and T.M. Jones. 2019. "Instrumental Stakeholder Theory Makes Ethically-based Relationship Building Palatable to Manag-ers Focused on the Bottom Line," *Academy of Management Review* 44, pp. 698–700. T.M. Jones, J.S. Harrison, and W. Felps. 2018. "How Applying Instrumental Stakeholder Theory Can Provide Sustainable Competitive Ad-vantage," *Academy of Management Review* 43, pp. 349–70; R.E. Freeman, J.S. Harrison, and A.C. Wicks. 2007. *Managing for Stakeholders: Survival Reputation and Success* (London, UK: Yale University Press).

21. J.S. Harrison, D.A. Bosse, and R.A. Phillips. 2010. "Managing for Stake-holders, Stakeholder Utility Functions and Competitive Advantage," *Strate-gic Management Journal* 31, pp. 58–74.

22. D.A. Bosse, R.A. Phillips, and J.S. Harrison. 2009. "Stakeholders, Reciproc-ity and Firm Performance," *Strategic Management Journal* 30, pp. 447–56.

23. B.R. Barringer and J.S. Harrison. 2000. "Walking a Tightrope: Creating Value through Interorganizational Relationships," *Journal of Management* 26, pp. 367–403; R.E. Freeman and W.M. Evan. 1990. "Corporate Gov-ernance: A Stakeholder Interpretation," *Journal of Behavioral Economics* 19, pp. 337–59.

24. Jones et al., "Instrumental Stakeholder Theory."

25. R.L. Priem, R. Krause, C. Tantalo, and A. McFadyen. 2019. "Promoting Long-Term Shareholder Value by 'Competing' for Essential Stakeholders: A New, Multi-sided Market Logic for Top Managers," *Academy of Manage-ment Perspectives*. doi.org/10.5465/amp.2018.0048.

26. W.J. Henisz, S. Dorobantu, and L.J. Nartey. 2014. "Spinning Gold: The Fi-nancial Returns to Stakeholder Engagement," *Strategic Management Journal* 35, pp. 1727–48; J. Choi and H. Wang. 2009. "Stakeholder Relations and the Persistence of Corporate Financial Performance," *Strategic Management Journal* 30, pp. 895–907; R. Sisodia, D.B. Wolfe, and J.N. Sheth. 2007. *Firms of Endearment: How World-Class Companies Profit from Passion and Purpose* (Upper Saddle River, NJ: Wharton School Publishing); A.J. Hillman and G.D. Keim. 2001. "Shareholder Value, Stakeholder Management, and Social Issues: What's the Bottom Line?" *Strategic Management Journal* 22, pp. 125–39; L.E. Preston and H.J. Sapienza. 1990. "Stakeholder Manage-ment and Corporate Performance," *Journal of Behavioral Economics* 19, pp. 361–75.

27. R. Garcia-Castro and C. Francoeur. 2016. "When More Is Not Better: Complementaries, Costs and Contingencies in Stakeholder Management," *Strategic Management Journal* 37, pp. 406–24; Jones et al., "Instrumental Stakeholder Theory."

28. J.S. Harrison and D.A. Bosse. 2013. "How Much Is Too Much? The Limits to Generous Treatment of Stakeholders," *Business Horizons* 56, pp. 313–22.

29. Some of the material in this section is from J.S. Harrison, D.B. Bosse, and S.B. Tallman. 2017. "Resource Creation Systems." Presented at the annual meeting of the Strategic Management Society, Berlin.

30. R.E. Freeman, R. Phillips, and R. Sisodia. 2020. "Tensions in Stakeholder Theory," *Business & Society* 59, 217.

31. F.E. Kast and J.E. Rosenzweig. 1972. "General Systems Theory: Applications for Organization and Management," *Academy of Management Journal* 15, pp. 447–65; D.M. Rousseau. 1979. "Assessment of Technology in Organizations: A Closed Versus Open Systems Approach," *Academy of Management Review* 4, pp. 878–96.

32. Kast and Rosenzweig, "General Systems Theory."

33. Penrose, *Growth of the Firm.*

34. T.J. Rowley. 1997. "Moving Beyond Dyadic Ties: A Network Theory of Stakeholder Influences," *Academy of Management Review* 22, pp. 687–910.

35. Kast and Rosenzweig, "General Systems Theory."

36. Penrose, *Theory of the Growth of the Firm.*

37. S.S. Zumdahl. 2005. *Chemical Principles.* 4th ed. (New York, NY: Houghton Mifflin Company).

38. T.M. Smith and R.L. Smith. 2015. *Elements of Ecology.* 9th ed. (Upper Saddle River, NJ: Pearson).

39. J. von Liebig. 1840. *Organic Chemistry in Its Application to Agriculture and Physiology* (London, UK: Playfair).

40. M. Bowe, K. Vonatsos, and S. Zarkos. 2005. "Decision Rules for Allocating a Limiting Factor Across Products in a Stochastic Production Environment: A Real Options Approach," *Accounting and Business Research* 35, pp. 183–205.

41. D. Albert, M. Kreutzer, and C. Lechner. 2015. "Resolving the Paradox of Interdependency and Strategic Renewal in Activity Systems," *Academy of Management Review* 40, pp. 210–34; E. Deming. 1994. *The New Economics* (Cambridge, MA: Massachusetts Institute of Technology).

42. L.A. Broedling. 1999. "Applying a Systems Approach to Human Resource Management," *Human Resource Management* 38, p. 270.

43. W.R. Scott and G.F. Davis. 2007. *Organizations and Organizing: Rational, Natural, and Open System Perspectives* (Upper Saddle River, NJ: Pearson/Prentice Hall).

44. Harrison et al., "Managing for Stakeholders."

45. Bosse et al., "Stakeholders, Reciprocity and Firm Performance."

46. D.J. Teece. 2014. "The Foundations of Enterprise Performance: Dynamic and Ordinary Capabilities in an (Economic) Theory of Firms." *Academy of Management Perspectives* 28, pp. 328–52; Teece et al., "Dynamic Capabilities and Strategic Management."

47. T.S. Cho and D.C. Hambrick. 2006. "Attention as the Mediator between Top Management Team Characteristics and Strategic Change: The Case of Airline Deregulation," *Organization Science* 17, pp. 453–69.

48. Teece, "Foundations of Enterprise Performance."

CHAPTER 3

Strategic Direction: Mission, Vision, Core Values, and Business Model

High-performing companies tend to have an organizational purpose that is understood by both internal and external stakeholders. This purpose is defined in terms of what it stands for, the stakeholders it serves, what it provides to those stakeholders, and how value is provided to them. When these things are put into writing, they become parts of the mission, vision, core values, and business model of the organization—the components of strategic direction.

A well-defined and widely communicated strategic direction helps stakeholders know what to expect and, thus, helps guide their decisions. For example, customers get a sense of the types of products and services the firm produces as well as their quality and the level of service they might expect after the initial sale. Employees and managers—as members and, thus, representatives of the firm—use strategic direction as a foundation for making decisions about what the firm expects them to do in a variety of situations. Communities, financiers, and suppliers get similar signals and can thus make better decisions about how (or if) to engage in transactions with the firm. In this regard, it is important to note that all firms have a strategic direction even if it is not communicated in formal documents. However, putting strategic direction into writing helps with both consistency and communication.

This chapter could be positioned later in the book. In terms of sequence in the strategic planning process, firms often collect information through strategic analysis before they go back and revisit their strategic direction to determine if their mission and business model are still reasonable or need to be revised. However, because strategic direction is the foundation for all the other topics, it is discussed early in this book. Basically, managers need to determine the overarching purpose of the firm and its general approach for achieving it before they are able get into more details about specific strategies.

Mission and Vision

One of the most common means to communicate strategic direction is a written mission statement. An organization's mission provides an important vehicle for communicating its ideals and a sense of direction and purpose to internal and external stakeholders. It can also help guide organizational managers as they make decisions, including choices about how resources are allocated.

Sometimes there is confusion between the terms *mission* and *vision*. In general, an organizational mission is what the organization is, whereas a vision is a forward-looking view of what the organization wants to become. Often a vision is expressed in terms of an aspiration to be the best in an industry at doing something, thus, providing superior value to particular stakeholders, such as the firm's customers. For example, the Bank of India has a vision to be the preferred bank for its target customer groups.[1]

Vision statements are not always published separately from mission statements. Frequently, they are embedded in the formal mission statement. In fact, a written mission statement may include a vision, definition of the business, and even the values a firm aspires to follow. The labels a firm uses for its written documents are not nearly as important as including all of the essential elements of strategic direction in them. In one form or another, a firm should define what it is and what it is trying to become, including a definition of its business and what it strives to do for its key stakeholders. The mission statement of UPS summarizes these things fairly well:

Grow our global business by serving the logistics needs of customers, offering excellence and value in all that we do. Maintain a financially strong company with broad employee ownership that provides a long-term competitive return to our shareowners. In-spire our people and business partners to do their best, offering opportunities for personal development and success. Lead by ex-ample as a responsible, caring, and sustainable company making a difference in the communities we serve.[2]

Note that UPS defines its business as logistics and its market as global in scope. In addition, the firm specifically mentions employees, share-holders, business partners, customers, and communities. The values of excellence, caring, responsibility, and sustainability are also included in the statement.

Many organizations prominently display their mission statements or print them on identification cards or key chains for their employees. If top managers are not deliberate in the process of communicating the mission to internal stakeholders, they will have no positive effect on the behavior of these stakeholders. In addition to providing direction for internal stakeholders, written mission statements are also often a way of communicating with the public. For example, mission state-ments are frequently included in annual financial reports, press releases, or letters to various stakeholders. Since they are public relations tools, they should be carefully crafted and concise enough so that people will actually read them. However, creating a mission or vision statement should not be an exercise in slogan writing. Some managers worry more about writing a catchy, short phrase that can be printed on a business card than about managing with purpose. Mission and vision statements should have real meaning and accurately reflect the direction of the organization. Research indicates that firm performance is influenced by whether a firm is authentic—acts in a manner that is consistent with its *stated* values.[3]

Core Values

The *core values* of an organization define what matters when making deci-sions and what is rewarded and reinforced. They are a practical applica-tion of business ethics. For instance, if an organization puts a lot of value on treating stakeholders with respect, then, presumably managers and employees who behave accordingly will be acknowledged and rewarded. Core values help a firm define its purpose in answering the fundamental question, "What do we stand for?" They help to determine the way stakeholders are treated and the importance they are given in the decisions a firm makes. As in the UPS example, sometimes core values are incorporated into mission statements. However, separate core value statements have become increasingly popular in recent years, partially as a response to highly publicized corporate scandals and stakeholder legal suits.

Honda's core values are a fascinating combination of aspiration and ethics. They include dreams, joy, a challenging spirit, passion, and respect. The company describes dreams as follows:

> To dream is to be alive. Dreams define who we are, forming a positive driving force that motivates us. They cause us to imagine what could be, to seek out challenges, and to be unafraid of failure. Dreams are our commitments to future generations.[4]

Core values statements can help organizations resolve *ethical dilemmas*, which occur when the values of different stakeholders of the organization are in conflict over a particular issue. For example, a firm may be trying to decide whether to close an unprofitable plant. The employees, union (if applicable), and surrounding community would be expected to resist the closing, but financiers and shareholders may favor it. The firm's core values help to determine whether issues of trust, good faith, and moral obligation are raised when decisions are being deliberated and the degree to which they influence the final outcome. This is not to say that plants should never be closed. However, a firm with stakeholder-based values would be expected to consult with employees, union representatives, and community leaders first to gain their perspectives on how the plant might be changed so as to make it profitable or, if it is closed, how to minimize the negative impact.

Employees and managers face decisions every day that have ethical implications: whether to tell a customer the truth that the customer's order will be shipped late, whether to exaggerate a travel expense claim for a particularly inconvenient business trip, or whether to ship a marginal product as first quality in order to meet the daily output quota. Although some of these decisions concern personal honesty more than business practice, the organization's core values help determine how employees deal with them. The key is to create and sustain an ethical climate in which managers and other employees behave ethically as a matter of routine.[5]

High-level managers, especially CEOs, have a great deal of influence on the core values of an organization and whether they are considered authentic. Managers who work with a CEO quickly identify her or his value system and communicate it to lower level managers and employees. The CEO may also discuss organizational values in speeches, news releases, and memos. To the extent that the CEO controls the rewards systems, managers who make decisions that are consistent with the CEO's values are likely to be rewarded, thus reinforcing what is expected. Many of the people who strongly disagree with the core values will leave the organization voluntarily or they will be forced out through poor performance evaluations, missed promotions, and/or low salary increases. Thus, over a period of time, the CEO's example and actions are reflected in most of the major decisions that are made by the organization.[6]

Business Model

A business model helps distinguish a firm from its competitors in terms of the way it intends to grow and create value for its customers and other stakeholders. A mission statement may contain elements of a business model, but it will not contain sufficient detail to guide a firm's operations. There is no consensus in the strategic management literature on the definition of a business model or what it contains. This book envisions the five essential elements of a business model as (1) a definition of the market segments the firms is attempting to serve, (2) the way in which assets are utilized, (3) the value proposition the firm is pursuing within its chosen markets, (4) the manner in which value is captured by the firm to sustain its value creation system, and (5) basic growth strategies (see Figure 3.1).

Market

Market definition:
- Broad market
- Focus on particular market or markets

Assets

Assets sold:
- Physical products
- Services
- Financial assets
- Intangible assets

Rights to assets transferred:
- Complete transfer
- Distribution of assets created by others
- Rights to use assets for specified time
- Broker (match buyers and sellers)

Value Creation

Unique sources of value:
- Differentiation (unique features embedded into assets; higher price)
- Low cost (basic products, services, or other assets at a low price)
- Best value (some differentiation but accompanying emphasis on lowering costs keeps prices down)

Value Capture

Method(s) for capturing some of the value created for customers
- Sales of product and services
- Sale of information or technology (e.g., patents)
- Lease or rental revenues
- Broker or subscription fees
- Advertising fees
- Franchise fees

Basic Growth Strategies

Internal growth
- Market penetration (increase sales volume w/existing products)
- Market development (new market segments for existing products)
- Product development (new products or product modifications for new or existing markets)

External growth
- Alliances/joint ventures
- Acquisitions (all or part of company)

Internal or external
- Vertical integration

Figure 3.1 Defining a business model

Definition of Market

One important element of a firm's business model is the extent to which it attempts to serve the needs and wants of a particular segment of its market. A firm that does so is pursuing what is called a *focus* strategy. A firm like Toyota has diversified its product line such that it is apparent that the company is pursuing a very broad consumer market. Contrast Toyota's approach with that of Porsche, which focuses on a very specific group of consumers. The amount of focus a firm pursues is important to guiding specific decisions regarding how the firm will execute its business model. Products and services are tailored around the needs and wants of the target customers and internal resources are allocated accordingly. Marketing is also directed at those customers, and information about them is collected on a continuing basis. The firm pays special attention to these relationships.

The extent to which a firm focuses on specific customers or targets a broad swath of the market is important to the firm's strategy, but it does not define how those customers will be served. The basic approach to the "how" question is found in decisions about the nature of assets sold and the value proposition the firm presents to its customers.

Disposition of Assets

Another important element of a business model is determining the types of assets a company sells and the rights it gives to consumers who use those assets. A firm may sell physical assets (i.e., products), human assets (i.e., services), financial assets (i.e., cash, securities), and/or intangible assets (i.e., patents, knowledge/technology). In terms of the rights a company provides, a company may create and transfer the rights to entire assets, such as products; distribute products made by others; sell the right to use assets for a specific time (i.e., a hotel room, intellectual property); or simply receive a fee for matching buyers and sellers (e.g., a broker).[7]

Value Proposition

Firms produce products and services that provide value to their custom-ers. There are two primary ways firms do this.[8] They may focus on products or services that are different from those of competitors, where those differences are valued by customers (e.g., novel designs, higher quality, unique features). This is called a *differentiation strategy*. Alternatively, they may emphasize production of basic products and services, produced at a lower cost and usually offered at a much lower price. This is a *low-cost leadership strategy*. In addition, some firms pursue a combination of the two options, a hybrid competitive strategy called *best value*. A well-defined value proposition, also referred to as a firm's *business-level strategy* or simply its *business strategy*, helps managers make strategic decisions regarding resource allocations, helping the firm to meet customer needs in ways that competitors do not, thus creating a competitive advantage and superior financial returns for the firm. Any number of firms might be pursuing the same broad strategy, but they would tend to pursue it in different ways and with varying degrees of success.

Differentiation Strategy

In differentiation strategies, the emphasis is on creating value through uniqueness. Uniqueness can be achieved through product innovations, superior quality, or superior service, which is then sustained and leveraged through creative advertising, brand building, and strong stakeholder relationships. Apple is a clear example of a firm following a differentiation strategy. The company offers very high quality, innovative products at a premium price. Although cost may not be their primary focus, firms pursuing differentiation strategies cannot ignore their cost positions. When costs are too high relative to competitors, a firm may not be able to recover enough of the additional costs through higher prices. Therefore, a differentiator must carefully manage costs across its entire production process from idea inception to delivery, but particularly in those areas that are not directly related to the sources of differentiation.

A differentiation strategy will lead to higher firm performance only if buyers value the attributes that make a product or service unique enough to pay a higher price for it or if they choose to buy from that firm preferentially. If most customers are willing to sacrifice some of the features, services, or reputation associated with a particular product or service in favor of a lower price, the strategy will fail. Also, even if a firm is successful at differentiating its products or services, it is likely to become the target of the imitative efforts of competitors. As competitors imitate, the formerly differentiating features will become commonplace and no longer the basis for a differentiation claim. Rivalry in an industry can make it very difficult to sustain a competitive advantage from any one innovation for very long. Consequently, staying ahead of the competition in product development requires *constant* innovation.

Low-Cost Leadership Strategy

Firms pursuing low-cost leadership set out to become the lowest cost providers of a good or service. One example is Walmart. An obsession with cost helped the company become the largest retailer in the world. Walmart developed a highly efficient distribution system using large, strategically placed warehouses and technology. The size of the company provides economies of scale, and Walmart puts pressure on its suppliers to drop their prices so that the savings are passed on to the consumer. Employees are paid relatively low wages, and work schedules emphasize efficiency.

Generally, low-cost leadership allows a firm to compete by lowering prices when needed without becoming unprofitable. When the demand for products and services exceeds the available industry supply, a low-cost leader will be able to price its products at the average industry price and still reap larger profits than competitors. When there is an excess of supply, competitors will drop prices to win customers, and the low-cost leader will be able to secure a small profit even when competitors are losing money. Consequently, low-cost leaders may be better positioned for economic downturns than companies pursuing other types of strategies.

Firms pursue low-cost leadership through a variety of tactics. One of these is high capacity utilization. When customer demand is high and the firm's capacity (floor space, employees, equipment) is fully utilized, fixed costs are spread over more units, which lowers unit costs. This concept is just as relevant for hospitals, retail stores, and software developers as it is for manufacturing plants. This basic concept suggests that a firm capable of maintaining higher levels of capacity utilization, through either better demand forecasting, conservative capacity expansion policies, or aggressive pricing to generate purchases or transactions, will be able to maintain a lower cost structure than a competitor of equal size and capability.

Another tactic for keeping costs low is making use of the efficiencies associated with mass production. Economies of scale are often confused with increases in the *throughput* of a manufacturing plant or other facility. As described earlier, increases in capacity utilization that spread fixed expenses can lead to lower unit costs. However, true economies of scale are cost advantages associated with larger sized facilities rather than with increased volume through an existing facility. For example, the cost of constructing a 200-bed hospital should not be twice the cost of building a 100-bed hospital, all other things held equal, so the initial fixed cost per unit of capacity will be lower. Not all larger facilities or manufacturing operations are more efficient. In fact, diseconomies of scale occur when a firm builds facilities that are so large that the sheer administrative costs and confusion associated with the added bureaucracy overwhelm any potential cost savings.

Learning effects can also help a firm achieve lower costs than its competitors, especially when the firm is introducing a product or service that is new or significantly modified. Learning effects occur because a firm gains experience as it produces more of the product or service, and this experience is translated into more efficient ways to produce it. Consider, for example, a firm that produces a new hand-held electronic device, or at least a device that is different enough from what currently exists that it can be considered a significant innovation. The first few devices (prototypes) are very expensive to produce. However, as the device is put into production on a larger scale, the per unit cost typically drops significantly. As more units are produced, the cost per unit drops even more, up to a point at which costs per unit tend to level off. Learning effects can explain why firms are often willing to experience a loss on a product when they begin selling it. They try to keep costs as low as possible to build market share so that they have an efficiency advantage over competitors.

Learning effects are related to the concept of a first mover advantage, which accrues to a firm that brings a new or significantly altered product or service to the market before competitors. However, first mover advantages are usually discussed as a marketing phenomenon and tend to be closely related to things like consumer awareness or loyalty. On the other hand, learning effects are more closely aligned to production efficiency.

A firm can, of course, experience both sources of advantage simultaneously when they are first to market.

Firms that pursue low-cost leadership are also prone to invest in research and development leading to cost-saving technologies. Companies that make investments in cost-saving technologies are often trading an increase in fixed costs for a reduction in variable costs. While investments of this type are typically associated with the factory floor, it is just as common for investments to be made in office and service automation. For example, the automated distribution system at Walmart, Internet banking services and reservation systems all represent investments in technology that serve to lower overall costs and provide a degree of information and control that was previously impossible.

Companies that are able to achieve high capacity utilization, economies of scale, and/or economies of technology may have the lowest cost, but do not have to charge the lowest price. In other words, a *low-cost* leader does not have to be a *price* leader. If a firm is able to achieve the lowest cost, but charge a price that is the same as that of competitors, it will enjoy higher profits. However, this approach entails some risk because there is no price incentive for customers to select its product over another. If customers are lured away to other brands, the loss of sales could reduce capacity utilization, reduce learning and experience effects (because the total volume produced would increase at a slower rate), or undermine scale benefits. As is the case with all strategies, the success of the low-cost leadership strategy is a function of supply and demand in the marketplace, the needs and preferences of customers, the capabilities and actions of competitors, and the effectiveness of the firm's strategy execution.

Best Value Strategy

In today's intensely competitive global marketplace, some of the most successful organizations in the world have successfully combined pursuit of both lower costs and differentiation. Rather than envisioning differentiation and low-cost leadership as two ends of a spectrum, it may be better to think of both as foundation accomplishments that must be reinforced and improved over time as part of the iterative, ongoing strategic management process. Successful differentiation makes the product more attractive to the market, which leads to volume increases. Then, as volume increases, management has the opportunity to employ the cost drivers noted earlier (capacity utilization, economies of scale, learning, automation) to drive down unit costs. Earnings that come from lower costs can then be reinvested into new forms of differentiation and cost efficiency. Consequently, this strategy is called *best value* because it provides a reasonable trade-off between low cost and differentiating features.

As Toyota has demonstrated and analysis has proved, the highest levels of product quality and reliability can be complementary with low cost.[9] Technological investments often allow firms to lower their costs while improving their performance on features that differentiate the company's products or services in the eyes of customers. Internet banking services and debit/ATM cards improve access and availability of teller services while reducing direct labor costs. A well-designed website can provide more detailed, easy-to-access information to customers at much lower cost than staffing teams of service operators.

A best value strategy can be understood in terms of supply and demand economics. For example, assume that three organizations manufacture digital watches. The first firm pursues a low-cost strategy. It is able to produce a basic watch for $10 and sell 100,000 a year at $20, for a total profit of $1 million. The second firm uses a differentiation strategy. It produces a premium watch with high-tech features that the market finds attractive. The premium product costs $40 to make. The firm can sell 50,000 at $60. The total profit is also $1 million, although the unit volume is half that of the low-price competitor. Both companies are successful; yet, they are each achieving success using a different strategy.

Now assume that a third company can create a very good watch, through a variety of product and process technological advances, for $20. Suppose also that this product is almost as appealing as the product of the second firm. If the firm can sell 75,000 at $50, the total profit will be over $2 million and consumers will believe they are getting a great deal (saving $10). This is the essence of a best value strategy—finding a level of differentiation that will bring a premium price while doing so at a reasonable cost.

International Product/Market Strategy

Organizations that are involved in multiple international markets may have advantages available to them in pursuing their business models. For example, firms that seek to improve their competitive position through low-cost leadership may choose to purchase materials or components from lower cost international suppliers, subcontract the assembly or manufacture of their products to international companies with lower labor and overhead costs, or purchase finished products from international companies for branding and resale in the home country. In addition to the cost advantages derived on the supply side, companies may pursue international markets as a way to increase their volume and secure cost advantages associated with volume and scale. International involvement may also help a company advance its competitive strategy of differentiation through means such as licensing advanced technology from abroad, distributing high-value imported products at a premium price in the domestic market, or growing an international brand for a premium domestic product by selling into high-end international markets.

One of the key issues facing top managers as their organizations pursue international strategies is determining the degree to which products and services should be customized to meet unique customer demands. If customers in nations and regions of the world have different needs or make purchase decisions in very different ways, then it will make sense to create products and services that address those specific needs. This approach, called a *multidomestic* product/market strategy, involves custom tailoring products and services around individual market needs and may involve conducting the design, assembly, and marketing on a country-by-country or region-by-region basis. Most fashion products, some furniture items and home appliances, and some entertainment products are developed and sold on this basis. Multidomestic strategies are intuitively appealing from a stakeholder point of view because they emphasize the satisfaction of segmented customer needs. However, customization may add more costs to the products or services than can be successfully recaptured through higher prices.

On the other hand, some products appeal to the entire global marketplace as is, which means one product design can be marketed throughout the world. This *global* product/market strategy is typical of steel and other commodity materials, as well as many electronic components and devices. Economies of scale may be available to firms pursuing this strategy because production can be centralized in one geographic location.

Some organizations are now pursuing a hybrid *transnational* product/market strategy that combines the efficiencies of the global strategy with the local responsiveness of the multidomestic strategy. For example, auto manufacturers tend to engineer model lines with features that are found in a large number of vehicles, but then they custom tailor many of the details to suit particular international markets. The transnational approach is sometimes also called *glocalization.*

Value Capture

One of the important characteristics of open systems is that they need regular infusions of resources from their external environments in order to survive. A business firm, as an open system, often sells its products and services as a primary method of obtaining the revenues it needs so that essential resources can be acquired. This is its value capturing mechanism. Other value capture options may include sales of information or technology (e.g., patents), lease or rental revenue (i.e., hotels, rental cars, building leases), broker or subscription fees, advertising fees, or franchise fees. Bartering is another technique for capturing value that may not necessarily involve the direct exchange of money. A firm exchanges a product or service it has for a product or service it needs. Of course, many such exchanges would still be taxable, which means that the firm would have to establish an exchange price on the basis of the fair market value of the exchange. Although a larger existing firm may have already established a successful method of value capture, it is sometimes fruitful to explore new options for value capture that might provide additional revenues.

Careful selection of the method or methods of value capture is especially important for entrepreneurial ventures, whether they are brand new firms or new ventures within an existing firm.[10] Consider the case of an Internet startup that is providing a web-based service. It has been determined through strategic analysis that there is demand for the service, and the firm has also figured out which features are most desirable to the target customers. The firm still has to determine how it will capture the revenues it will need to survive, grow, and achieve profitability. Many web-based firms raise revenues through charging for advertising, but there are so many already established websites competing for advertising dollars that often a new venture will be unsuccessful with this method. Some of these firms capture revenues through monthly fees or on a fee-per-service basis. Others may have to give their service away for free for a time so as to establish a presence on the Internet. This is possible if the venture is well funded, which may be difficult to do. Eventually, every business needs to resolve successfully the value capture issue in order to survive.

Basic Growth Strategy

Firms use a variety of methods to grow. Among the *internal growth strategies, market penetration* is the most conservative. A firm pursuing this type of growth tends to invest a lot in marketing as a vehicle to increase demand for its existing products and services. Research and development is limited, and the firm is most likely to be engaged in a low-cost leadership strategy based on economies of scale or high capacity utilization. A *market development* strategy also focuses on existing products and services, but the firm attempts to enter new market segments. Finally, *product/ service development* involves the creation of new products for both new and existing markets. Successfully pursuing this strategy involves substantial commitments to both research and development and marketing, as well as changes to the firm's *value chain*, which pertains to the processes through which the firm converts resource inputs into consumable products and services.

External growth strategies can involve a variety of forms of *alliances and joint ventures* with external stakeholders such as customers, suppliers, universities, government agencies, and even competitors. These growth strategies are often pursued because a firm lacks a particular resource or capability it needs. In addition, a firm may use *acquisitions* as a way to grow instantly while obtaining the needed knowledge or other resources it lacks for its value creation system. These external growth strategies will be discussed extensively in later chapters: alliances and joint ventures will be discussed in Chapter 6 and acquisitions will be covered in Chapter 8.

For now, it is prudent to point out that although they can be very beneficial to a firm, and they certainly stimulate growth, they are difficult to orchestrate successfully and very risky.

Church & Dwight Co., makers of Arm & Hammer products, is a good example of how a basic growth strategy can develop over time. Starting in the 19th century, its sodium bicarbonate product (baking soda) was used in recipes and as a cleaning agent. However, Church & Dwight then began marketing its baking soda as a deodorizer (specifically, for refrigerators), thus opening another market segment (market development). In the wake of national criticism of laundry detergents containing phosphates around 1970, Church & Dwight seized the opportunity and, in less than a year, developed a new phosphate-free detergent that was the first to market (product/service development). Beginning at the turn of the last century, Church & Dwight began making a series of acquisitions of other consumer product companies. Today the firm has a diversified portfolio of products, including oral hygiene products, laundry detergents and prewash additives, pain relievers, vitamins, and hair products.[11] The company even acquired Agro BioSciences, Inc., a high-tech research and development company that specializes in animal health.

Vertical integration is another basic growth strategy. It can be pursued through internal means as a firm begins to manufacture components that it used to buy from external suppliers (backward integration) or starts using its own products in the next stage of its value chain (forward integration). As an example of forward vertical integration, a firm that makes electronics and sells them to retail outlets might open its own retail stores. As another example, a firm that makes parts that it sells to lawn mower manufacturers could begin to manufacture its own lawn mowers. Vertical integration can also be pursued through joint ventures in which the firm partners with another firm to vertically integrate or through an acquisition in which a firm buys one of its suppliers or a company to which it sells its products or services. While vertical integration has intuitive appeal, in reality it often involves getting into a business about which the firm's managers know very little. More will be said about vertical integration in Chapter 8.

International Growth Strategy

A final element of a firm's strategic direction is its international growth strategy. Some firms choose to remain domestically focused, while the potential for growth through international expansion is appealing to others, especially if competition is fierce in the home country or there is high growth in demand for particular products and services in other countries. Firms apply a variety of expansion tactics as they pursue global opportunities. Among the most common are the following:

1. *Exporting*: The firm transfers goods to other countries for sale, often through wholesalers or a foreign company
2. *Licensing*: The firm sells the right to produce and/or sell a brand-name product in a foreign market
3. *Franchising*: A foreign firm buys the legal right to use the name and operating methods owned by a foreign firm in its home country
4. *Joint Venture*: A cooperative agreement among two or more companies to pursue common business objectives in countries in which they are not currently engaged.
5. *Greenfield Venture*: The creation of a wholly owned foreign subsidiary—the firm buys the assets required, hires the people, builds and runs the operation, acquires the necessary government permits, and so forth

Some of the most important criteria when deciding on an option for international growth are cost, financial risk, profit potential, and control. In general, moving down the list of alternatives from one to five entails not only greater cost and greater financial risk but also greater profit potential and greater control. Consequently, these alternatives represent a trade-off between cost and financial risk on the one hand and profit and control on the other. Of course, this is a generalization. Some of the options, such as joint venture, are hard to judge on the basis of these four criteria because the exact nature of the agreement can vary so widely from venture to venture.

What Strategic Direction *Should* Be

As this chapter has demonstrated, there are many elements involved in a firm's strategic direction. Although it might require significant effort, it is worth it to spend the time reviewing a firm's current direction and discussing *what it could be and what it should be*. Often changes to one or various elements of a firm's strategic direction come as a result of strategic analysis and strategic assessment, which are discussed in the next three chapters.

As suggested at the beginning of this chapter, a well-devised and widely communicated direction provides guidance to internal stakeholders—managers and employees. It helps them understand how to make decisions that will further the purposes of the firm and that are also consistent with its basic strategies. It reduces confusion and motivates higher levels of performance. A clear and widely disseminated strategic direction can also provide valuable information to external stakeholders such as customers, suppliers, and the communities in which firms operate. It can help draw stakeholders to a company, motivate them to engage in behaviors that facilitate the creation of more value, help them anticipate how the firm is likely to behave, and both anticipate and understand the decisions of its managers.

Notes

1. Bank of India. n.d. "Our Vision." https://bankofindia.co.in/MissionVision1, (accessed October 15, 2019).
2. Mission Statement Academy. 2019. "Mission Statement."http://mission-statement.com/ups/, (accessed October 15, 2019).
3. M. Cording, J.S. Harrison, R.E. Hoskisson, and K. Jonsen. 2014. "Walking the Talk: A Multi-stakeholder Exploration of Organizational Authenticity, Employee Productivity, and Post-Merger Performance." *Academy of Management Perspectives* 28, no. 1, pp. 38–56.
4. Honda. "Honda's Core Values," http://discover.honda.com/pdf/Honda-Core-Values.pdf, (accessed October 15, 2019).
5. T. Thomas, J.R. Schermerhorn, Jr., and J.W. Dienhart. 2004. "Strategic Leadership of Ethical Behavior in Business," *Academy of Management Executive* 18, no. 2, pp. 56–68.

6. K. Adelman. 2012. "Promoting Employee Voice and Upward Communication in Healthcare: The CEO's Influence," *Journal of Healthcare Management* 57, no. 2, pp. 133–47; A. Mackey. 2008. "The Effect of CEOs on Firm Performance," *Strategic Management Journal* 29, pp. 1357–67.

7. P. Weill, T.W. Malone, and T.G. Apel. 2011. "The Business Models Investors Prefer," *MIT Sloan Management Review* 52, no. 4, pp. 16–19.

8. This discussion of business strategies draws heavily from concepts found in M.E. Porter. 1980. *Competitive Strategy: Techniques for Analyzing Industries and Competitors* (New York, NY: The Free Press), Chapter 2; see also Harrison and St. John, *"Foundations,"* Chapter 5.

9. N. Shirouzu and J. Murphy. 2009. "A Scion Drives Toyota Back to Basics," *Wall Street Journal*, A1, A4; M. Walton. 1990. *Deming Management at Work* (New York, NY: G.P. Putnam's Sons).

10. M. Roessler, V.K. Velamuri, and D. Schneckenberg. 2019. "Corporate Entrepreneurship Initiatives: Antagonizing Cognitive Business Model Design," *R&D Management* 49, pp. 509–33.

11. Church & Dwight. n.d. "Our History." https://churchdwight.com/company/history.aspx, (accessed October 16, 2019).

CHAPTER 4

Strategic Analysis of the Value Creation System: Internal Resources and the Value Chain

An open systems approach to the strategic management process requires ongoing collection of information about the firm's value creation system, each of the components of that system, and the environment in which it exists. Although the precise components of each firm's system may vary, the primary components are illustrated in Figure 4.1. Internal analysis, pictured in the middle of the figure, includes evaluation of the firm's resources for their potential as sources of sustainable competitive advantage. It also includes financial resource analysis and evaluation of employees, managers, and the governance structure of the firm. This chapter also discusses the firm's value chain, the system through which supplies enter the firm, are converted into products and services, and are subsequently sold to customers. A firm's value chain is at the core of its value creation system. The rest of Figure 4.1 will be covered in Chapter 5, including competitive (e.g., industry) influences, community and financier influences, secondary stakeholders (i.e., special interests, regulators, media, trade unions), economic forces, sociocultural forces, political forces, and technological forces.

It is important to understand from the outset that there are *two* essential takeaways from the analysis process described in this chapter and Chapter 5. First, internal resource analysis is intended to help a firm determine which of its resources, if any, are sources of *sustainable*

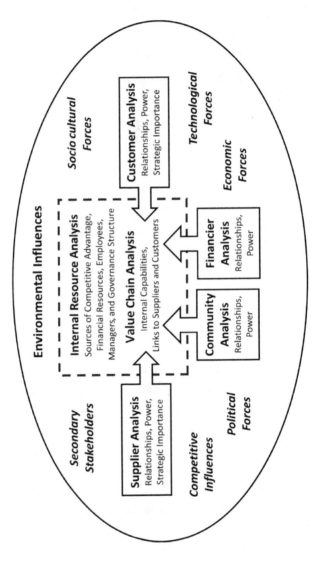

Figure 4.1 Primary components for strategic analysis of a firm's value creation system

competitive advantage—an advantage-providing resource that is very expensive or otherwise extraordinarily difficult to imitate. An internal resource analysis might also help a firm determine areas of weakness in its value chain, but that is not the primary intent of this sort of analysis. The rest of the analysis tools contained in these chapters are intended to help a firm with the second takeaway, which is determining which area(s) of a firm's value creation system could be holding back the creation of additional value for stakeholders. Even if the firm has a resource or multiple resources that provide sustainable competitive advantage, this analysis is useful because a firm can still improve its value creation system by identifying and improving weak areas in its system. Also, a firm's value creation system requires constant adjustment to deal with changes that occur in the external environment.

While Chapters 4 and 5 provide a lot of analysis tools, these chapters contain only limited insights regarding how to use the information they provide to improve the firm's ability to create value for stakeholders. However, Chapter 6 will provide a practical set of tools that utilize the information obtained through analysis to create or adjust firm strategies, guide decisions, and allocate resources and managerial attention.

Real systems are messy, so there is overlap between the components of a firm's value creation system. For example, the internal resources that will be evaluated during the resource analysis are also part of the firm's value chain. However, it is important to remember that the two types of analysis have different objectives. Also, there is significant overlap between environmental influences such as sociocultural forces and economic forces, in addition to commonalities among political forces, communities, and secondary stakeholders. This sort of overlap is evident throughout the analysis chapters and is no reason for concern. What is most critical to a strategic analysis is to make sure that all the essential components are included, and not to focus on how they are categorized.

Analysis of Internal Resources

Chapter 2 introduced the idea that competitive advantage may be available to firms that possess valuable resources and capabilities. A firm may possess superior human, financial, physical (i.e., plants, products, locations), knowledge and learning, or general resources (i.e., reputation, stakeholder relationships, culture, organizational structure, patents, and brands and trademarks). Alternatively, it is also possible that a firm may not possess any extraordinary resources and still be highly competitive because of the effectiveness of its value creation system. Nonetheless, this section is about how to identify those resources and capabilities, if they exist, that do lead to a competitive advantage. This sort of information can be valuable to managers so that they can protect the value of the resource and give it sufficient attention during planning processes. Also, managers might find new ways to utilize the resource to make the entire value creation system more effective. In addition, managers might devote attention to developing a new resource as a source of sustainable competitive advantage if the firm does not already possess any that have the essential characteristics.

Sustainable Competitive Advantage

There are several conditions that make a resource or capability a genuine source of sustainable competitive advantage. Of course, to be a source of *sustainable* competitive advantage a resource must first be a source of competitive advantage. This requires the following:

1. The resources or capabilities are *valuable*: The term *valuable* is used in a market sense. In general, market value comes from the ability to use the resource to provide a good or service at a lower cost *or* to provide a good or service that is more desirable to the consumer.
2. The resources or capabilities are *unique*: If numerous organizations possess a particular resource or capability, then the situation is described as *competitive parity*—no company has the advantage. On the other hand, if only one organization, or a small group of organizations, possesses a valuable resource or capability, then that resource or capability may be a source of competitive advantage. Rareness also implies that there are not readily available substitutes for the resource or capability. This would be something that could be used in its place without a loss of value, such as substituting with a different type of computer application, medicine, or production process that achieves approximately the same end result.

3. The *organization* is suited to the exploitation of the resource or capability: This means that the structure and systems of the firm are appropriate for taking advantage of the resource or capability. For example, Nokia, once dominant in the cell phone market, declined rapidly in spite of huge investments in research that led to many cutting-edge discoveries. Nokia's inventions did little to help the company because its research efforts were fragmented and disconnected from the operations that could have brought these products to market.

4. The firm's managers are *aware* of the potential of the resource or capability to lead to a competitive advantage and have taken steps to realize the advantage: In other words, they have acted on the information about the competitive potential of a resource or capability.

   Turning a competitive resource or capability into one that is a *sustainable* source of competitive advantage requires the following additional condition:

5. The resources or capabilities are *extremely difficult or very expensive to imitate*: In these situations, competing firms face a cost disadvantage in imitating a resource or capability. The more difficult or costly a resource or capability is, the more valuable it is in producing a sustainable competitive advantage. One of the biggest difficulties new Internet businesses encounter is that their resources and capabilities tend to be widely available and not hard to imitate.[1]

If a resource or capability has all of these characteristics and it can also be applied to more than one business area within the same company, it is called a *core competency*, or may also be called a *distinctive competence*. Some companies are masters at exploiting their sources of competitive advantage across different businesses. For example, Disney has a core competency in creativity that allows it to extend its unique and valuable animated characters, which were created in its studios, into a multitude of businesses, including books, movies, theme parks, and television. Walmart has a core competency in using logistics management techniques, resulting in a world-class distribution system that is difficult to imitate.

That said, it is becoming increasingly difficult for firms to develop or acquire resources and capabilities that provide *sustainable* competitive advantages.[2] Fast-paced competition, technological advances, and a rapidly changing global environment mean that a resource that is providing a competitive advantage at present may become outmoded or irrelevant in a short period of time. For example, a new feature on a smart phone or a new service in a hotel chain may provide a competitive advantage for a short time, but competitors will soon imitate it. This is especially true for *tangible resources*, which are resources that can be seen, touched, easily explained, and/or quantified.[3] Because of their tangibility, they tend to be easy to imitate. Examples include existing products, machinery, plants, simple technologies, or access to raw materials.

Intangible resources, on the other hand, are more difficult to imitate. They include research capabilities that are tied to specific individuals or groups of individuals within the firm, processes that lead to innovation or efficiency, relationships between the firm and important stakeholders, organizational culture, and managerial capabilities. Because they are among the most difficult resources to imitate, *intangible resources have a high potential to lead to sustainable competitive advantage.*

One of the keys to high performance resulting from resource and capability advantages is combining resources to develop capabilities that are hard to imitate. For example, while a patent, which is tangible, may provide an organization with a competitive advantage for a while, the capability to quickly develop and introduce attractive new products provides an even more secure source of competitive advantage. It involves integrating the efforts of several resources: marketing, research and development, operations, and many others. Integrated resources and capabilities are particularly difficult for competitors to imitate. Of course, these types of resources and capabilities may rely on most or even all of a firm's value creation system, as opposed to only one part of it. One implication of this sort of interconnectedness for managers is that none of the resource areas can be neglected.[4] If one of them becomes weak, it can influence all of the other resource areas. Also, it is important to seek ways to connect various parts of the system in unique ways to develop competencies that are difficult to imitate. Some of the resource areas a firm should evaluate for their competitive potential will now be examined.

Financial Resources

Analysis of financial resources is a powerful tool for both internal resource analysis and, as will be discovered later in this chapter, value chain analysis. This is because financial figures pertain to so many parts of a firm's value creation system. A few popular financial figures and ratios that are useful in evaluating financial trends, making comparisons with competitors, and assessing various parts of the firm's value creation system are found in Table 4.1.

Financial resources can themselves be a source of advantage, although they rarely qualify as *unique* or *difficult to imitate*. Nevertheless, a strong cash flow, low levels of debt, a strong credit rating, access to low-interest capital, and a reputation for creditworthiness are strengths that can serve as a source of strategic flexibility in that they allow a firm greater freedom to enhance its value creation systems, develop new products and services, and satisfy stakeholders. Among other things, financial analysis is used to indicate the ability of the firm to finance growth. For example, managers of a firm that has a very high leverage (long-term debt) may have to be less ambitious in their strategies for taking advantage of opportunities. On the other hand, an organization with a strong balance sheet is well poised to pursue a wide range of opportunities. Strong financial resources are often hard to imitate in the short term.

Financial analysis is also an important strategic tool used by managers in assessing firm performance and identifying strengths, weaknesses, and trends. In general, financial analysis involves making two essential comparisons: (1) a comparison of the firm with its competitors, to determine relative financial strengths and weaknesses, and (2) a comparison of the firm with itself, over time, to show trends.

Firms often attempt to compare their expenses, investments, sources of income, and resulting profitability with those of their competitors as a way of assessing the success of their strategies. A firm may observe that competitors are making more aggressive investments in research and development (R&D) or paying higher wages to employees, which may heighten competitive intensity in the future. The findings from a competitor comparison must always be weighed against the goals of the firm. For example, a firm's investment in inventories may be higher than that

Table 4.1 Useful financial information for trend analysis and competitor comparisons

Strategic information		
R&D intensity	R&D expenditures/Sales	Emphasis on innovation
Advertising intensity	Advertising expenditures/Sales	Emphasis on marketing; level of product/service differentiation
Capital intensity	Capital expenditures/Sales or Capital expenditures/Assets	Anticipated growth or modernization efforts
Employee compensation	Wages or total employee compensation/Sales	Dependence on labor; may also be one indication of employee treatment
Efficiency/Activity		
Labor force efficiency	Sales/Number of employees or Payroll expenses/Sales	Efficiency of workforce
Asset turnover	Sales/Total assets	Efficiency of asset utilization
Inventory turnover	Cost-of-goods-sold/Average inventory or Sales/Average inventory	Ability to control investment in inventory
Gross profit margin	Sales *minus* Cost-of-goods-sold/Sales	Efficiency of operations and product pricing
Growth in sales	(Sales at end of year *minus* Sales at beginning of year)/Sales at beginning	Success of marketing strategy; popularity of products and services
Liquidity/Leverage		
Current ratio	Current assets/Current liabilities	Short-run ability to meet financial obligations; financial slack
Quick ratio	(Current assets *minus* Inventories)/Current liabilities	Short-term liquidity; financial slack
Debt-to-equity	Total liabilities/Shareholder's equity	Relative amount of debt and equity financing; financial risk
Debt ratio	Total liabilities/Total assets	Percentage of assets financed through borrowing; financial risk
Profitability/Overall financial performance		
Return on Assets (ROA)	Net profit after taxes/Total assets	Productivity of assets
Return on Equity (ROE)	Net profit after taxes/Shareholder's equity	Earnings power of equity
Earnings Per Share	Net profit after taxes/Number of common shares outstanding	Earnings of each share of outstanding stock; large impact on share price
Total Return to Shareholders	(Share price at year end *minus* Share price at beginning of year + Dividends per share)/Share price at beginning of year	Amount each shareholder earned on a share of stock; share price appreciation only realized with sale of stock

of competitors for one of three reasons: (1) it is not as effective at managing inventories as competitors, which would be a cause for concern; (2) higher levels of inventories support its particular strategy (e.g., fast delivery and guaranteed availability); or (3) the items in inventory or accounting conventions are different, making it a meaningless *apples and oranges* comparison.

Firms also track their own expenses and sources of income, over time, as a way of identifying trends. Poor financial trends are sometimes symptoms of greater problems. For example, a firm may discover that administrative costs are increasing at a faster rate than sales. This could be an indication of diseconomies of scale or the need for tighter controls on overhead costs or, on the contrary, part of a deliberate attempt by the firm to position itself now for future sales growth.

Employees

Employees and the way they are recruited and managed can be important sources of competitive advantage. For example, Starbucks devotes a lot of attention to its human resources. The company is very selective in its recruitment programs and invests in its employees to make sure they are as competent as possible. This has allowed the company to do most of its management recruiting from within. The company also provides a high level of employee benefits. This sort of treatment has led to unusually high levels of employee satisfaction and motivation in an industry that is known to be one of the worst employers.

Firms that treat their employees well are investing in the future because employee retention is likely to be higher. Furthermore, firms may expect higher levels of productivity due to higher motivation levels and commitment among their employees.[5] Some programs, such as educational benefits, provide immediate advantages to the firm because employees bring new ideas and improved skills to the workplace. Also, the best potential employees are drawn to firms that have a reputation for excellent employee treatment.

Analysis of human resources should include an examination of trends in critical areas. Employee turnover by type of employment (i.e., administration, office, sales, production, etc.) and organizational level is one of the most important areas to evaluate because a lost employee means also a loss of recruiting, training, and experience resources. High levels of turnover can also hurt the morale of the employees who remain. Some other important metrics could include sales per employee, compensation per employee, absenteeism rate, training levels, and experience levels of employees.[6] Also helpful is a survey of employees to determine levels of satisfaction with various elements of their job (including process and supervision issues) and to ask for their feedback on how to improve the job as well as the value creation process. For example, an employee survey could ask about new opportunities for products and services to satisfy the needs of customers or how processes within the firm might be improved. In addition, external sources can be a good source of information on how well the firm is doing in the human resources area. For example, *Fortune* publishes a list annually of the best companies to work for.

In addition to evaluating how experienced, motivated, and satisfied employees are, firms can also determine the amount of economic power they have. Powerful employees can have a greater influence on their employment contracts, including wages, benefits, working conditions, schedules, and bonuses. In general, employees are more powerful under the following conditions:

1. *Shortages* exist in the areas where the firm needs them.
2. The *skill and experience levels of employees are differentiated*, and the firm needs workers with particular skills and experience in order to carry out chosen strategies and achieve firm objectives.
3. Competitors are aggressively seeking to *hire away skilled employees* with attractive employment offers.
4. Employees have sufficient *information about the operations of the firm*, its costs, production methods, and profitability levels to negotiate an attractive employment contract.
5. It is *expensive, difficult, or time consuming to train employees* to a level at which they become productive parts of the value creation system.
6. Employees are represented by a *union*, or they pose a credible threat of becoming unionized if they are not treated well.[7]

An effective employee analysis can help identify sources of both strength and weaknesses in the firm's value creation system. This information is then used in strategy development. For instance, a firm that is weak in recruitment or training may need to create a strategy that overcomes these weaknesses in order to achieve a higher level of value creation in its system. Alternatively, a firm with very well-trained and loyal employees may have more flexibility with regard to the types of strategies it can consider. In addition, assessing the power of employees is useful in determining expectations regarding employment conditions and costs and, as will be explained in Chapter 6, whether employees are being given sufficient attention and resources.

Managers and the Governance Structure

Talented and experienced managers can also be a source of competitive advantage.[8] Some of the same sorts of analysis tools that were used for employees can be applied to managers. Of course, there are also some traditional financial measures that can be applied to rate the efficiency of a particular operation, such as comparisons of actual results with allocated budgets for sales or expenses or an examination of growth trends for a particular area over which a manager has control. When tracked over time, these sorts of measures can be very helpful. However, they should not be relied on exclusively to determine how well a manager is doing. The nature of relationships between a firm and stakeholders (internal and external) is often dependent on interactions between those stakeholders and a particular manager. It is useful to ask stakeholders about the managers they interact with to complete the picture. This sort of information can be obtained through surveys (online is easiest) or private contacts between stakeholders and managers higher in the hierarchy.

Research has shown that top managers can have a significant impact on the strategies and performance of their organizations.[9] The highest ranking officer in a large organization can be called by a number of titles, but the most common is *chief executive officer*, or CEO. The CEO has primary responsibility for setting the strategic direction of the firm (see Chapter 3), although larger organizations are typically led by several high-ranking officers, such as chief operating officers and vice presidents, who form the top management team.

Because of the complexity of environmental forces and the need to manage relationships with a diverse group of stakeholders, top management teams need a variety of strengths, capabilities, and knowledge. A *heterogeneous top management team* is made up of managers with a wide variety of functional backgrounds, education, and experience.[10] Members of a heterogeneous top management team benefit from discussing issues from a wide variety of perspectives. These discussions can improve the quality of firm decisions. Heterogeneity is also positively associated with innovation and strategic change. Nevertheless, in spite of these advantages, heterogeneity can also make implementing a strategy more difficult, in part because of communication difficulties resulting from managers who have very different perspectives and cognitive skills.[11]

Most larger organizations, and especially those that have issued stock, have a board of directors. Boards can also be a valuable resource to organizations. They play an important role in governing the behavior of top managers, determining their compensation, ensuring that the organization is acting ethically and legally, and protecting the interests of key stakeholders. However, board members can also play other important strategic roles, such as providing advice to managers with regard to strategies and strategic direction. If a board of directors is composed of highly successful executives from a range of industries, it will be able to provide a broader perspective to top management. Also, directors can provide social network ties, which act as linkages to external stakeholders. For example, a board interlock occurs when a director or executive of one firm joins the board of another firm. *Interlocking directors* can lead to transfer of knowledge and experience among firms, including information about strategies, structures, and organizational systems and processes.[12] Firms often appoint subsets of the board of directors into working committees so that they are better able to focus on the specific issues at hand. Some of the most common are audit committee, nomination committee, and executive compensation committee.

There is some variation with regard to governance structure across countries. For example, the United States has a single-tier system, with a board of directors elected by the shareholders. In some other countries, such as Germany and Austria, a two-tier system exists, with a management board of executive directors and a supervisory board composed entirely of nonexecutives.[13]

Because not all managers have a personal financial interest in the firm they are managing (e.g., own stock), the potential for conflict of interest exists. That is, it is possible that a manager might do something for his or her own benefit at the expense of other stakeholders, such as the shareholders. Toward the end of the last century, management scholars began to embrace what is called *agency theory* to explain these sorts of conflicts.[14] According to agency theory, top managers are agents for the shareholders—they are obligated to act in the shareholders' interest. One line of thinking even suggests that managers have a legal obligation to act in the shareholders' best interest, although there is evidence that this is not the case.[15]

When managers attempt to maximize their own self-interest at the expense of shareholders' interest, an *agency problem* is said to exist. For example, a CEO might have the firm make a poor acquisition to enhance her or his own power and control even though it would end in lower returns for the shareholders. In reality, both managers and directors should feel an obligation to protect the interests of *all* the firm's legitimate stakeholders—those that participate in the value creation processes of the firm. Shareholders are one of the stakeholders whose interests should be protected, but so are employees, customers, suppliers, and communities. They all have a vested interest in the outcomes of the firm due to their contributions to value creation.

Highly vigilant boards are widely regarded as the best defense against conflict of interest.[16] These are boards that pay attention to what the firm is actually doing. They use their rights to determine compensation or fire irresponsible executives as leverage to ensure that they are acting in the best interests of stakeholders and also in accordance with applicable laws and regulations.

One highly publicized method that companies have used to increase the ability of their boards to monitor the actions of top management has been to include a majority of nonemployee directors (outsiders) on their boards. These types of boards are called *independent*. In recent years, boards of the largest U.S. companies have become more independent.

However, there is inconclusive evidence on whether board independence is actually associated with higher firm performance, at least during normal circumstances.[17] The composition of the board of directors seems to make more of a difference in crisis situations, such as bankruptcies or takeovers, perhaps because firms rely more on their boards during these difficult times.[18]

Incentive compensation is another mechanism that directors use to encourage CEOs and other high-level executives to act in a responsible manner, especially on behalf of the shareholders. For example, firms may provide CEOs with stock or stock options, which are contracts that allow a CEO to purchase stock at a future time at a price that will be attractive if the company performs well. In large corporations, it is not unusual for noncash compensation to be greater than the cash portion of a CEO's total annual compensation. Use of stock or stock options encourages managers to focus on shareholder returns because their own compensation is dependent, in part, on those returns. Some corporations also require directors to hold stock in the company, which further aligns their interests with the shareholders.

An analysis of top management and governance includes examination of structural elements, such as board composition, as well as any evidence that managers are acting in their own best interests at the expense of the greater good. Among other things, exorbitant compensation relative to executives in similar positions, decisions that enhance the power or position of a CEO but seem to hurt firm performance, or excessive perks may be evidence of an agency problem that could be hurting the entire value creation system.

This completes the section on analysis of internal resources. Internal resource analysis provides guidelines for understanding which firm resources might be providing competitive advantages for the firm and which of them might also be sustainable over time. This sort of analysis can also expose which of the resources is weak and could thus be holding back the firm's entire value creation system. Analysis of a firm's finances is also a powerful tool to help determine strengths that a firm can exploit as well as weak areas associated with parts of the firm's value creation system that could be holding back the whole system. Firms can examine internal trends to look for symptoms of deficiencies that may exist in particular areas and should also compare these figures with those of close competitors to the extent such information is available. This section also provided examples of tools that are useful in analyzing employees and the management and governance structures of the firm.

Analysis of the Value Chain

Thus far we have examined the firm in terms of its internal resources and capabilities, as well as its financial and human resources and its governance structure. Figure 4.2 contains a model of what is often called a *value* chain, which is at the core of a firm's value creation system.[19] A value chain includes all of the processes that work together to create the products and services that provide value for customers. Consequently, much of what was discussed in the last chapter can be applied to analysis of the value chain, in addition to identifying sources of competitive advantage. However, this section focuses specifically on basic value chain activities as well as the activities that support them. In addition, suppliers and customers, as principal parts of the value chain, will be examined in this section. *Logistics* is the term most often used to describe coordination of value chain activities. By examining a firm's value chain, managers can identify key resources and processes that represent strengths to be exploited, as well as areas that could be holding back the firm's entire value creation system.

Basic Value Chain Activities

The basic activities of the value chain include upstream value chain management, internal operations management, distribution and physical location management, marketing management, and management of post-transaction contacts. *Upstream value chain management* includes activities associated with acquiring resources that are used to create the product or service the firm provides to its customers. For manufacturers, these processes include activities such as purchasing raw materials and other factors of production, warehousing, materials handling, and inventory control. Some service organizations, such as financial or consulting firms, may not need to acquire or manage a lot of raw materials, but they still

Basic Value Chain Activities

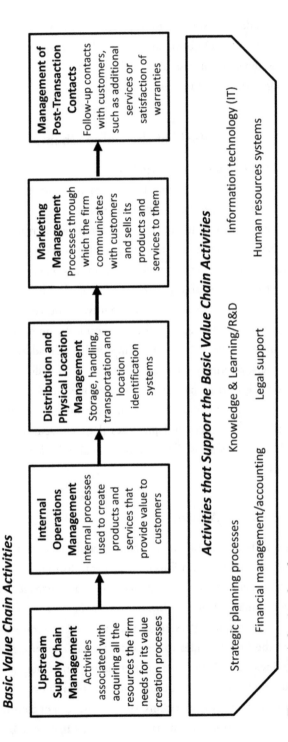

Upstream Supply Chain Management
Activities associated with acquiring all the resources the firm needs for its value creation processes

Internal Operations Management
Internal processes used to create products and services that provide value to customers

Distribution and Physical Location Management
Storage, handling, transportation and location identification systems

Marketing Management
Processes through which the firm communicates with customers and sells its products and services to them

Management of Post-Transaction Contacts
Follow-up contacts with customers, such as additional services or satisfaction of warranties

Activities that Support the Basic Value Chain Activities

Strategic planning processes   Knowledge & Learning/R&D   Information technology (IT)

Financial management/accounting   Legal support   Human resources systems

Figure 4.2 A firm's value chain

make purchases to support their operations. The most successful Japanese auto manufacturer, Toyota, is a master of inbound logistics. Many of its suppliers are located very close to its factory, and Toyota keeps very little inventory of the components it uses in its vehicles; instead, it has a working arrangement with suppliers so that the components it needs arrive *just in time* for use on its assembly lines.

One measure of the performance of the inbound logistics system is *raw materials turnover*, which can be measured as a ratio of cost-of-goods-sold to average raw materials inventory. The firm can also examine the costs associated with obtaining, storing, handling, and transporting these resources, as a percentage of cost-of-goods-sold or simply against prior years. Also included should be an assessment of the quality of the inputs acquired, the firm's ability to obtain what it needs on a timely basis, and relationships with suppliers.

Internal operations management refers to transforming inputs into final products and services. For manufacturing firms, this involves activities such as machining, assembly, molding, testing, and printing. In service firms, activities might include cooking (for restaurants), baggage handling (for airlines), or cleaning rooms (for hotels).

There are many ways to assess the efficiency and effectiveness of internal operations. Table 4.1 contains a few financial metrics that are helpful in this regard, including growth in sales (an indication that products and services are pleasing to customers), R&D intensity, gross profit margin, asset turnover, and inventory turnover. Overall measures of efficiency include ratios such as cost-of-goods-sold to sales, cost-of-goods-sold to total employee expenses (or production employee expenses), administrative expenses to cost-of-goods-sold or sales, cost-of-goods-sold or sales to the value of fixed assets (market value or depreciated property, plant, and equipment). Many companies also look at defect rates within their production systems or return rates from customers. Also, the employee and management analyses described previously in this chapter can be very helpful tools in evaluating internal operations. This is not a comprehensive list. These are merely examples. Every firm should develop its own metrics to evaluate how well its internal operations are working. Basically, there are many production systems within this part of the value chain, and the more fine-tuned the measures, the easier it is to identify what might be holding back the creation of more value. Also, most larger firms are not one operation, but many, and each of those operations requires its own analysis.

Distribution and physical location management, for a manufacturing firm, pertains to activities related to storing and physically distributing the final product to customers, such as finished goods warehousing, order processing, and transportation. Finished goods inventory turnover (Sales/ Average finished goods inventory) is a useful metric for analysis in some manufacturing firms. Order processing and transportation costs can also be tracked, as a trend or proportional to cost-of-goods-sold or sales.

A key part of this activity is determining locations for the operations of the firm such that the distribution process is most efficient. The same holds true for service providers. Although service providers may not distribute a lot of physical goods to customers, which means they do not have to worry much about things like finished goods warehousing, they still have to decide where to put their operations so as to maximize the potential to create value for customers. In some instances, this means finding places from which the most customers can be served. For example, McDonalds is very skilled at finding the best locations for its restaurants. Many manufacturing and service firms have found that clustering near competitors creates an advantage.[20] In manufacturing, these firms share suppliers, distributors, and technology providers. They also have an advantage in recruiting highly skilled managers and employees because they also tend to cluster in those areas and often they don't even need to move when they change employers. For service firms, such as hotels and restaurants, clusters often draw in more customers. That is, customers go to that location specifically because of the variety and volume of service providers. Of course, service firms can also share suppliers.

Marketing management includes processes through which customers can purchase the product or service and through which they are induced to do so, such as website design, advertising and promotion, direct sales strategies, distribution channeling, and pricing. Marketing is a huge differentiator between successful and unsuccessful firms in industries such as beverages, insurance, restaurants, and apparel. Companies like Coke, Geico, and Nike give a lot of attention and resources to marketing management.

Specific to marketing, inventory turnover and advertising intensity (see Table 4.1) are useful metrics, especially when a firm compares its figures to those of close competitors. However, while advertising intensity measures the amount of financial resources a firm devotes to advertising, it does not measure effectiveness. Several options exist today to assess that effectiveness, many of which are web based. Third party providers offer services in which they track consumer perceptions of brands, products, and services. A firm can also conduct its own research to learn how consumers view the company and what it offers. Marketing research through focus groups, online or mail surveys, and personal interviews is absolutely critical to keeping a firm and its products and services innovative and appealing. This sort of research might also be classified under the support area called *knowledge and learning*, which will be examined in the next section. Remember that it is not so important where critical activities are analyzed, but that they are all included in an analysis of a firm's value creation system.

Finally, *management of post-transaction contacts* refers to providing services to enhance or maintain product value. For firms that sell products, this may involve making adjustments to the product, supplying parts, installation, or satisfying a warranty. For both product and service firms, activities may include simply following up to answer questions or ensure customer satisfaction. Amazon.com is well known for its incredible service after the sale. The company goes out of its way to satisfy customers who experience a problem with what they have bought.

There are a variety of ways to measure the effectiveness of these activities in the value chain; however, the simplest and probably most effective way is to simply ask customers. Also, in many cases, it is the service or follow-up after the sale that helps determine whether a customer will seek the firm first for future purchases. Consequently, measures of repeat business can be helpful in assessing this area.

Support Activities

Organizations also engage in numerous activities that support these value-creating functions, displayed at the bottom of Figure 4.2. Note that a firm's strategic planning processes helps to coordinate all of the basic and support activities as well as provides direction to the firm as it determines future strategies for creating additional value. These processes are essential to managing all parts of a firm's value creation system, of which the value chain is the major part.

The firm's *knowledge and learning activities* are also critical to the entire value creation system. More than 50 percent of the gross domestic product in many developed economies, including the United States, is based on intangible skills and intellectual assets. Organizational learning, of which R&D is a part, is closely connected to all of the other resource and value chain areas. Firms that lose their ability to innovate quickly wear down and become less competitive either because of a lack of efficiency (production innovation) or because its products and services seem outdated to customers (product/service innovation).

Organizational learning involves (1) knowledge creation, (2) knowledge retention, (3) knowledge sharing, and (4) knowledge utilization.[21] Knowledge creation requires effective R&D programs, as well as an organizational climate that encourages discovery. In addition, an abundance of knowledge is available through tapping what primary stakeholders already know and through examination of published research studies and the actions, processes, and publications of competitors. Retention of information is also a priority. Information technologies such as low-cost data storage devices, the Internet, and cloud computing have made it possible for firms to handle large volumes of information at a low cost. *Data analytics*, encompassing techniques for processing data to enhance productivity and innovation, has become an increasingly important function within many firms. Some of them are using data analytics to process *big data*, extraordinarily large data sets, to identify trends or patterns that are useful in guiding many aspects of their operations and marketing.

A firm's *information technology* (IT) encompasses all of the processes associated with collecting, analyzing, storing, and disseminating information within the firm. Having state-of-the-art IT is not sufficient for creating a sustainable competitive advantage. IT is simply a tool that must be managed effectively to facilitate the creation of resources, including knowledge and skills, that lead to competitive advantage.

Especially in industries that experience rapid change, attention to R&D is often critical to competitiveness. Table 4.1 contains an R&D Intensity measure that can be tracked as well as compared with competitors. Also, a declining gross profit margin or one that is lower than that of competitors could be a sign that the company is not innovative enough in its operations. Sales growth is one indicator of how innovative a firm's products and services are, especially compared with competitors' sales growth. Effective R&D programs result in the creation of knowledge that can be used to differentiate products or produce them more efficiently. However, as mentioned previously, a firm can also gain this sort of knowledge through interactions with stakeholders, especially if they have strong relationships with them. A firm that uses surveys, focus groups, and other means to gather information from customers and potential customers is conducting marketing research, and this sort of research is critical because it helps a firm excel in the marketing management function, the basic value chain function discussed previously.

Knowledge can be divided into two types: codified and tacit.[22] *Codified knowledge* can be communicated with precision through written means. It includes things like formulas, designs, and computer code. Codified knowledge is closely related to the concept of tangible resources that was described earlier in this chapter. *Tacit knowledge*, on the other hand, is difficult to describe with words. It tends to be associated with intangible resources and capabilities, such as creative processes. You have to experience them to know how they work.[23] Tacit knowledge can be a valuable source of competitive advantage because it is very difficult to imitate. For example, although it might be possible to imitate a computer chip made by Intel, it would be nearly impossible to imitate the creative processes that resulted in the creation of the chip.

Financial management and accounting are also important to the firm's value creation system. In this regard, a firm might look at factors such as the following:

1. The timeliness and accuracy of financial reporting (including outcomes from audits)
2. Whether managers have the financial information they need when they need it
3. The cost of administering the finance and accounting functions and whether that cost is increasing
4. Whether there are any problems with regulatory compliance
5. The interest costs of old and new debt
6. Leverage and liquidity trends and comparisons with competitors

There is not much to say about *legal support*, except that it is vital to have sufficient expertise in this area so that the firm can keep its reputation intact with stakeholders and avoid work stoppages, legal fines and payments, or other inefficiencies due to legal difficulties. One of the themes of this book is that firms that manage for stakeholders should need less legal support because they are less likely to upset stakeholders.

Finally, much of the analysis of the *human resources* support area pertains to the employee analysis discussed previously. Skill levels of employees, compensation and rewards systems, and promotion policies all relate to employee motivation, productivity, and turnover. If productivity is declining or does not compare well with that of competitors, or turnover is high, it may be evidence that human resource management systems need to be improved. Similarly, assessments of other relational factors, such as trust, cooperation, the quality of communications, and employee satisfaction, provide barometers of these systems.

For all of these components of the value chain, comparisons with competitors can be very meaningful in determining whether a particular part of the system is holding back the efficiency or effectiveness of the whole value creation system. Some of the information is available publicly or can be obtained through industry associations, financial analysts, research firms, or estimation based on the knowledge of managers and employees or their contacts with other firms. Other information is, unfortunately, unavailable. However, even in those cases, it may be possible, through observations of outcomes, to get some sense of how a firm compares against its competitors.

Suppliers and Customers

Thus far the emphasis in this discussion of the value chain has been on processes over which the firm has a fair amount of control. However, both suppliers and customers are an integral part of the value creation system, and they can directly influence the outcomes of the firm. This is particularly true of powerful suppliers and customers. These types of stakeholders can have economic or political power, and often political power results in stronger economic power.[24]

Political power comes from the ability of a stakeholder to influence the political process in its favor or against the firm. One type of political power is opinion leadership, the ability to sway public opinion about a firm. Stakeholders such as nongovernmental organizations (NGOs) and community activists have a certain degree of political power because they can influence public opinion. However, any of a firm's stakeholders may possess it. In addition, some firms are well positioned relative to other firms and enjoy an additional source of power as a result of what is called *network centrality*. For instance, a hospital system may have a strong network of close ties with regional doctors, medical equipment suppliers, and nonprofit medical research organizations. Finally, political power often comes from special relationships with politicians or government leaders within regulatory agencies. For example, a large supplier with strong ties to political leaders may actually have more political power than an activist. Stakeholders with political power can alter the firm's environment. To the extent that they influence government laws and regulations, they are altering the *rules of the game*, giving advantages to their own firm at the expense of others.

Economic power comes from the ability of a stakeholder to directly influence the economic outcomes of the organization. For example, powerful suppliers can exert influence and increase uncertainty for the buying industry by threatening to raise prices, reducing the quality of goods or services provided, or not delivering supplies when needed. In this sense, a stakeholder influences both the operating efficiency of the firm and the risk it faces. In general, supplier power (relative to the firm that is acquiring supplies from them) is greater under the following conditions:

1. Only a *few suppliers* exist to provide what the firm needs for its value chain and there are no genuine substitutes for what they provide.
2. The supplier *does not depend on the firm* for a lot of its sales.
3. A supplier has *differentiated its products and services* so that they are particularly appealing to the firm that is buying from it; this typically means that the products and services are essential to the value the firm creates.
4. A supplier can easily get accurate information on the buying firm's sales growth, costs, profits, and so forth. This is called *information asymmetry*. It gives them additional power during negotiations with the buying firm.
5. A supplier can *threaten to integrate forward* (and the threat is legitimate) and, thus, compete directly with its former buyer.

6. A supplier has made it *costly to switch* to other suppliers. For example, some manufacturers make products that work well with other products they make but do not work well with the products of other manufacturers, thus preventing buyers from switching.

7. A supplier has *preferential relationships or contracts* with other firms that make it difficult to compete. For example, a supplier may have an exclusive or long-term contract with another buying firm.

8. A supplier is *well connected politically*, which means that it can gain favorable treatment from government entities that is hard for the firm to match. Also, a well-connected supplier can influence legislation that is favorable to its side of transactions or threaten to do so if the firm does not yield to its conditions.

These forces combine to determine the economic strength of suppliers and the degree to which they can exert influence over the firm. Note that, as mentioned previously, the political power of a supplier (aforementioned condition number 8) enhances its economic power as well.

Although *all customers are important*, some have more economic power than others. Customers with high levels of economic power have a greater ability to dictate prices and other contract terms as they negotiate with sellers. Conditions that give customers economic power mirror those of suppliers. They include the following:

1. The firm has a *small number* of customers. In this case, losing one customer makes a big difference.

2. A customer makes *high-volume purchases*.

3. The products the customers are buying are *undifferentiated* (also known as *standard* or *generic*). This means that they are not concerned about which company they buy from.

4. A customer can easily get accurate information on the firm's costs and demand. This is also a form of *information asymmetry*, and it gives a customer additional power during negotiations with the selling firm.

5. Customers can *threaten to integrate backward* and become their own suppliers (and the threat is legitimate). This gives them the ability to threaten to quit buying from the firm.

6. A customer can *easily switch* from one seller to another at nominal or no cost.

7. A customer has *preferential relationships or contracts* with other firms that make it difficult to compete. For example, a customer may have an exclusive or long-term contract with another selling firm.

8. A customer is *well connected politically*, which means it can gain favorable treatment from government entities that is hard for the firm to match. Also, a well-connected customer can influence legislation that is favorable to its side of transactions or threaten to do so if the firm does not yield to its conditions.

In combination, these forces determine the bargaining power of customers—that is, the degree to which customers exercise active influence over pricing, other contract terms, and the direction of product development efforts. Large retailers, such as Walmart (based in the United States) and Carrefour (based in France), are powerful customers because they make very high-volume purchases and because of the ease with which they switch from one manufacturer to another for many products.

Analysis of the power of suppliers and customers is helpful for many reasons. It helps firms understand what to expect in negotiations with these critical stakeholders, and also provides guidance for how to manage relationships with them, one of the topics that will be covered in Chapter 6. However, it is also important to evaluate the nature of the relationships a firm has with its suppliers and customers. To what extent are these stakeholders cooperative with the firm? Do they freely share information and other resources, and does the firm reciprocate in sharing with those stakeholders? Are there any legal issues or other conflicts regarding contracts? Is there trust between the firm and its stakeholders? These sorts of questions can help a firm determine whether a relationship with a particular customer or supplier could be holding back the creation of more value.

Combining Internal Resource and Value Chain Analyses

A summary of the analysis of a firm's internal resources and value chain is found in Table 4.2. These analyses are powerful tools for assessing the state of the firm's competitiveness and the efficiency and effectiveness of its value creation system.

Table 4.2 Summary of analysis of a firm's internal resources and value chain

Component of value creation system	Objective	Examples of analysis tools
Internal Resources (human, financial, physical, knowledge/learning, general)	Determine which resources, if any, are sources of sustainable competitive advantage	Is a resource valuable, unique, inimitable? Is the firm organized to exploit the resource and are managers taking action?
Financial resources	Use financial information to diagnose which parts of system may be holding back value creation; identify financial strengths and weaknesses	Ratios and financial figures; trends and comparisons with close competitors; strategic, efficiency/activity, and profitability ratios
Employees	Assess whether weakness in employees is holding back value creation; assess employee power	Turnover trends, employee satisfaction, training and skill levels; factors that give employees power
Managers and governance structure	Evaluate management performance; determine if governance structure is optimal; look for agency problems	Compare budget to actual costs and sales; information from stakeholders; heterogeneity of top management team; management compensation; board independence; stock ownership of managers and board
Basic value chain activities	Evaluate components of value chain to determine if any may be holding back value creation in system; inbound logistics, internal operations, distribution and location, marketing, post-transaction contacts	Ratios, financial figures, defect rates, quality ratings, location desirability, customer surveys, third party research firms; comparisons with close competitors are especially helpful
Support activities	Determine whether activities that support the basic value chain activities are facilitating value creation	Assess innovation across entire system; effectiveness of technology and IT; surveys, focus groups; track administrative costs and cost of capital; financial audits
Suppliers and customers	Assess power and determine nature of relationships with key suppliers and customers	Power analysis on the basis of factors such as dependence, switching costs, product differentiation, political connections; examine levels of stakeholder cooperation, information sharing, reciprocity, trust, contract issues, complaints

It is possible that this chapter has seemed a little overwhelming; however, in order to provide a complete strategic analysis, a deep dive into the complexities of a firm's value creation system is necessary. Oversimplification would lead to unrealistic expectations regarding improving the firm's value creation system and performance. In reality, this chapter has only provided a solid start toward understanding aspects of a firm's value creation system that require tracking and analysis. Each firm will require other information depending on its own particular business situation. Remember that the end game is to use the information collected through analysis to improve the value creation system and, thus, create more value for stakeholders. After an examination of secondary stakeholders, communities, and the broad environment in the next chapter, Chapter 6 will provide guidance on how to use all of the information collected to help achieve this objective.

Notes

1. J.B. Barney. 1991. "Firm Resources and Sustained Competitive Advantage," *Journal of Management* 17, pp. 99–120; J.B. Barney. 1995. "Looking Inside for Competitive Advantage," *Academy of Management Executive* 9, no. 4, pp. 49–61.
2. R.A. D'Aveni, G.B. Dagnino, and K.G. Smith. 2010. "The Age of Temporary Advantage," *Strategic Management Journal* 31, pp. 1371–85.
3. M.A. Hitt, R.D. Ireland, R.E. Hoskisson, and J.S. Harrison. 2013. *Competing for Advantage*. 3rd ed. (Mason, OH: Thomson Higher Education).
4. D.G. Sirmon, M.A. Hitt, R.D. Ireland, and B.A. Gilbert. 2011. "Resource Orchestration to Create Competitive Advantage: Breadth, Depth and Life Cycle Effects," *Journal of Management* 37, pp. 1390–412.
5. G. Spreitzer and C. Porath. 2012. "Creating Sustainable Performance," *Harvard Business Review*, pp. 93–99; M. Subramony. 2009. "A Meta-analytic Investigation of the Relationship between HRM Bundles and Firm Performance," *Human Resource Management* 48, 745–68.
6. C.J. Capps, III, C.M. Cassidy, R. Gravois, and J.A. Warner. 2019. "Expanding the Competitive Profile Matrix: Introducing the Production/Operations Management, Marketing, Human Resource Management, Finance/Accounting, Research and Development, and Information Systems Competitive Profile Matrices," *Journal of Business Strategies* 36, pp. 59-–69.
7. R.E. Freeman, J.S. Harrison, and S. Zygliodopoulos. 2018. *Stakeholder Theory: Concepts and Strategies* (Cambridge, UK: Cambridge University Press), Chapter 5.

8. T.R. Holcomb, R.M. Holmes, Jr., and B. Connelly. 2009. "Making the Most of What You Have: Managerial Ability as a Source of Resource Value Creation," *Strategic Management Journal* 30, pp. 457–85.

9. A. Mackey. 2008. "The Effects of CEOs on Firm Performance," *Strategic Management Journal* 29, pp. 1357–67.

10. A.S. Alexiev, J.J. Jansen, F.A.J. Van den Bosch, and H.W. Volberda. 2010. "Top Management Team Advice Seeking and Exploratory Innovation: The Moderating Role of TMT Heterogeneity," *Journal of Management Studies* 47, pp. 1343–64.

11. W.B. Werther. 2003. "Strategic Change and Leader-Follower Alignment," *Organizational Dynamics* 32, pp. 32–45; C.C. Miller, L.M. Burke, and W.H. Glick. 1998. "Cognitive Diversity among Upper-Echelon Executives: Implications for Strategic Decision Processes," *Strategic Management Journal* 19, pp. 39–58.

12. C. Shropshire. 2010. "The Role of the Interlocking Director and Board Receptivity in the Diffusion of Practices," *Academy of Management Journal* 35, pp. 246–64.

13. R. Bohinc. 2011. "One or Two-Tier Corporate Governance Systems in Some EU and Non-EU Countries," *Megatrend Review* 8, no. 1, pp. 57–76.

14. M.C. Jensen and W. Meckling. 1976. "Theory of the Firm: Managerial Behavior, Agency Costs and Capital Structure," *Journal of Financial Economics* 3, pp. 305–60.

15. Stout, *Shareholder Value Myth*.

16. E. Fama and M.C. Jensen. 1983. "Separation of Ownership and Control," *Journal of Law and Economics* 26, pp. 301–25.

17. S.K. Lee and L.R. Carlson. 2007. "The Changing Board of Directors: Board Independence in S&P 500 Firms," *Journal of Organizational Culture, Communications & Conflict* 11, pp. 31–41; D.R. Dalton, C.M. Daily, A.E. Ellstrand, and J.L. Johnson. 1998. "Meta-analytic Reviews of Board Composition, Leadership Structure and Financial Performance," *Strategic Management Journal* 19, pp. 269–90.

18. S. Chatterjee, J.S. Harrison, and D. Bergh. 2003. "Failed Takeover Attempts, Organizational Governance and Refocusing," *Strategic Management Journal* 24, pp. 87–96.

19. This discussion of the value chain and Figure 4.2 were strongly influenced by M.E. Porter. 1985. *Competitive Advantage: Creating and Sustaining Superior Performance* (New York, NY: The Free Press), Chapter 2.

20. A.M. Hansson and K. Olofsdotter. 2013. "FDI, Taxes and Agglomeration Economies in the EU15," *Applied Economics* 45, pp. 2653–64.; L. Canina, C.A. Enz, and J.S. Harrison. 2005. "Agglomeration Effects and Strategic Orientations: Evidence from the U.S. Lodging Industry," *Academy of Management Journal* 48, pp. 565–81.

21. U. Lichetenthaler and H. Ernst. 2012. "Integrated Knowledge Exploitation: The Complementarity of Product Development and Technology Licensing," *Strategic Management Journal* 33, pp. 513–34; D.L. Deeds and D.M. DeCarolis. 1999. "The Impact of Stocks and Flows of Organizational Knowledge on Firm Performance," *Strategic Management Journal* 20, pp. 954–68.

22. D.J. Teece. 2000. *Managing Intellectual Capital* (New York, NY: Oxford University Press).

23. J.B. Barney. 2011. "Purchasing, Value Chain Management and Sustained Competitive Advantage: The Relevance of Resource-Based Theory," *Journal of Value Chain Management* 48, pp. 3–6.

24. This discussion of power is based on R.E. Freeman. 1984. *Strategic Management: A Stakeholder Approach* (Boston, MA: Pitman); M.E. Porter. 1980. *Competitive Strategy: Techniques for Analyzing Industries and Competitors* (New York, NY: The Free Press); J.S. Harrison and S.M. Thompson. 2015. *Strategic Management of Healthcare Organizations* (New York, NY: Business Expert Press), Chapter 4; R.E. Freeman, J.S. Harrison, and S. Zygliodopoulos. 2018. *Stakeholder Theory: Concepts and Strategies* (Cambridge, UK: Cambridge University Press), Chapter 5.

CHAPTER 5

Strategic Analysis of the Value Creation System: Environmental Influences

The last chapter focused on the firm's value creation system from the inside out. This chapter will discuss stakeholders and environmental forces that have an influence on that system—from the outside in. It is probably prudent at this point to repeat that the boundaries of the firm are not rigid, especially from a systems perspective. For example, customers and suppliers are often considered a part of the external environment because they are outside of the legal boundaries of the firm. However, as soon as the firm engages in transactions with them, they become a part of the firm's value chain, central to its value creation system. Similarly, communities in which the firm operates are primary stakeholders because they are a direct part of the firm's value creation system. Nonetheless, they are most often analyzed as a part of the external environment because their influence is similar to and often treated the same way as political and sociocultural forces.

As another example of the permeable nature of firm boundaries, although secondary stakeholders such as a nongovernmental organization (NGO) or an activist typically play an influencer role as a part of the external environment of a firm, sometimes a firm might engage directly with them, as in a situation in which an environmental group (i.e., the Sierra Club) cooperates with a land development company to select a location for a new plant. Another example would be when a representative of a consumer protection group is invited to become part of a firm's research and development project. These types of interactions defy what are thought of as traditional firm boundaries. Nonetheless, a more typical case is that the stakeholders and forces discussed in this chapter are treated s a part of the external environment. The chapter begins with a discussion of industry competition and economic forces.

Analysis of Competitive Influences

Competition has a huge influence on the success of a firm in achieving its purpose and on its performance. The intensity of competition in an industry is a function of a variety of factors such as sales growth and entry barriers. The power of competitors also determines the nature of competition, and, of course, the state of the economy provides the context in which industry competition occurs. An economy with strong growth can reduce the intensity of competition in an industry, whereas a stagnant economy intensifies it.

The Intensity of Competition

The intensity of competition can have a large effect on a firm's value creation system and the ability of the firm to achieve its objectives. Competition is more intense among competitors in industries characterized by the following:

1. There are a *large number of competitors*. This is rather obvious, of course, but the more competitors in an industry, the more the industry's sales must be divided.
2. The industry is *growing slowly*. A slowly growing industry means that sales growth often entails stealing market share from competitors.
3. The industry has a *high fixed cost* structure. If a firm has high fixed costs (i.e., huge plant, expensive machinery), there is a lot of pressure to meet particular sales levels in order to cover those costs. To the extent that rivals in the industry are facing the same sorts of costs, rivalry increases. This rivalry is often manifest in huge marketing campaigns and price discounting.
4. The products of the industry are *undifferentiated*. If the products of an industry are hard to differentiate, customers don't care much whose products they are buying. This means that there is a lot of pressure on prices, which often leads to price-cutting tactics.

5. *Barriers to entry are low.* These are factors that make it very difficult for a new firm to enter the industry, including economies of scale, highly differentiated products, limited access to distribution channels, and government policies and regulations that limit entry into an industry. Also, incumbent firms may possess resources that entering firms would find it difficult to obtain, such as patents, trade secrets, and special relationships or long-term contracts with particular stakeholders. When entry barriers are high, competition is reduced. When they are low, competition is increased because new firms enter regularly.

6. *Exit barriers are high.* High exit barriers mean that firms may lose all or most of their investments in the industry if they withdraw from it. Basically, their physical and intangible assets have little market value if they are used in any other application. Therefore, firms are more likely to remain in the industry even if profits are low.

7. *Many substitute products* exist for the goods and services provided by the industry. When organizations provide goods or services that readily substitute for those provided by other firms in the industry, then those organizations become indirect competitors. For example, milk, juices, and bottled water are all substitutes for soft drinks. Close substitutes can place a ceiling on the price that a firm can charge for a good or service, which can negatively influence profits.[1]

In some industries, competition is so intense that it is very difficult to earn a profit, as has been the case at various times in the airline, small electronics, grocery store, furniture store, and fast-food industries.

Information about the level and nature of competition in an industry is strategically useful because it allows a firm to develop strategies for its value creation system that may partially offset competitive influences. For example, a firm in an industry with a low level of differentiation might find creative ways to differentiate its products by developing a reputation for superior service or by creating an image for the product through advertising that makes it seem different to customers (i.e., Morton salt). Or a firm might erect entry barriers in an industry that has low barriers through exclusive long-term contracts with particular suppliers or customers or by lobbying the government to enact legislation that protects the industry (and thus the firm).

The Power of Competitors

One of the keys to a successful competitive analysis is to correctly determine which competitors are most likely to influence the firm's value creation system. Direct competitors can be defined as firms that compete for the same customers. PepsiCo is a direct competitor of The Coca-Cola Company. Target competes directly with Wal-Mart, and General Motors with Toyota, Honda, and Volkswagen. One of the inconsistencies found in the stakeholder literature is whether direct competitors are or are not treated as primary stakeholders. It is true that competitors have a stake in the firm in the sense that what the firm does matters to them, and vice versa. However, unless they are engaged in some sort of partnership or alliance with the firm, such as a lobbying group or a research project, they are not directly engaged in the firm's value creation system.

Instead of treating competitors as primary stakeholders, this book envisions a competitor as the orchestrator of its own value creation system, where their value creation system competes with the value creation system of the firm. For example, Nike's value creation system is in competition with that of Adidas in the athletic shoes and products industry. These two firms may share some stakeholders (i.e., customers, suppliers), but they are still competing systems. In most industries, competitive moves by one firm affect other firms in the industry, which may incite retaliation or countermoves. Competitors jockey with each other for market share, for the best employees, for capital, for the best supplies and locations, and even for the favorable comments of investment analysts. In many industries, every new product introduction, marketing promotion, and capacity expansion has implications for the revenues, costs, and profits of competitors.

Much like customers and suppliers discussed in the previous chapter, competitors vary in their power.[2] Powerful competitors can pursue strategies that harm the firm by taking away customers through means such as aggressive marketing campaigns and discounting, pursuing "first mover" advantages that make the products of competitors obsolete, or hiring away valuable employees. In general, the following conditions give competitors power:

1. They are *larger* than the firm. Larger firms possess more resources, enabling them to be more aggressive in their competitive tactics and to better weather any reciprocal actions from the firm. They may also enjoy advantages from economies of scale.

2. They possess *rare resources that are difficult or impossible to imitate*, such as unusually good locations, particularly well-trained or experienced employees, or technological advantages coming from patents or secrets.

3. Their *reputation* is exceptionally strong and is associated with brand name(s) and trademark(s) that are well recognized and have been established over a long time frame (i.e., Disney, Coke, Nike, Toyota).

4. They have *special relationships with stakeholders* that cannot be imitated completely owing to long-term contracts, exclusive partnerships, or permanent joint ventures. This is especially true if these relationships are with stakeholders that possess resources that are rare and hard to imitate.

5. They have *network centrality*, which means that they are leaders in a network of firms that work together to create value for stakeholders.

6. They are willing to pursue *aggressive strategies* that put competing firms at a disadvantage, even if these strategies are risky in that the outcomes are highly uncertain. Some people might call these firms mavericks.

7. They have strong *political connections*, which gives them the ability to influence legislation that changes the "rules of the game" (laws and regulations) and may also give them an advantage in selling their products and services to government entities.[3]

Analysis of the Community

The communities in which firms operate are primary stakeholders.[4] Many of the resources a firm uses in its value creation system come from local communities, and cooperation is required for a firm's value creation system to be efficient. Communities provide the local infrastructure needed for firms to operate, and many of a firm's stakeholders live close to the firm. Also, communities and their leaders influence the "rules of the game" through local laws, regulations, and taxes. Communities and their leaders generally have increased power under the following conditions:

1. Their *location is particularly well suited to the operations of the firm* because of access to suppliers, customers, raw materials and components, inexpensive labor, transportation, educational institutions, or for some other reason specific to the firm.
2. *Competitors have expressed an interest* in operating in the same community.
3. Community leaders enjoy the advantages of *information asymmetry* because it is easy to access information about the firm regarding sales, profits, policies, employment trends and wages, and environmental policies and actions.
4. The *firm is experiencing rapid growth,* and it is essential to expand operations.
5. *The tax structure or other laws and regulations* would be easy to change, and the changes could adversely influence the firm. For instance, this can happen if the local voters have a history of supporting such changes (e.g., a tax increase on local businesses).
6. The firm's *contracts in the local area are about to expire,* such as a lease of the land on which it operates.

Most communities welcome new firms into their areas because of potential economic impact. They may even offer tax incentives to expand there. However, once established in a community, power issues can have an influence on the relationship between the firm and local citizens and community leaders, which can have an impact on the firm's value creation system. For example, a community may demand changes to operations to conform to new environmental standards or changes to working conditions for employees.

Strong community relationships facilitate efficiency in the firm's value creation system. Therefore, in addition to analysis of power, community analysis should include an assessment of the nature of the relationships between the firm and the communities in which it operates. On the positive side, a firm can evaluate whether it has a favorable tax structure in the community (i.e., tax breaks or an attractive rate of taxation), generates positive news in the local press and social media, is considered a desirable employer by community members and their leaders, and is generally recognized as a good community citizen. Negative indicators may include bad press, negative social media, legal suits and fines, difficulty obtaining permits or licenses to operate or expand, or movements by community groups to alter the operations, priorities, or other business decisions of the firm.

Analysis of Financiers

Financiers such as banks and other financial institutions are primary stakeholders because they provide operating capital and other financial resources to support the firm's value chain. For example, they may help with the sale of bonds or stock. Financiers interact directly with the firm, and it is not unusual for their representatives to serve as advisors to the firm or on the board of directors, especially if the company is not particularly large. Financiers have more economic power under the following conditions:

1. *The industry in which the firm does business is unstable* because it is new, small, or engages in a business that is considered by some as socially questionable (e.g., gambling, alcohol, guns).
2. *Not many financiers* are interested in doing business in the industry.
3. *The firm is young* and does not have an established record of success.
4. The firm has experienced *financial difficulties in the past.*
5. The firm has *high leverage or low liquidity,* which makes it a riskier investment.[5]

Shareholders should not be left out of this discussion because they provide a lot of financial capital for the firm. They can exert a powerful force on the firm to the extent that they hold large amounts of stock. For example, a large investor such as a pension fund, mutual fund, or hedge fund frequently has a seat on the board of directors and can influence top managers to make decisions that they believe will enhance the value of their shareholdings. A discussion of the various tools large share-holders use to exert influence on the firm is beyond the scope of this small book. Small shareholders don't have much power, and must rely on the board and managers to protect their interests. Of course, a firm that neglects shareholder interests by providing a low or highly volatile return for shareholders over time will have a lower share price and experience difficulty raising more capital through future issues of stock.

Analysis of Secondary Stakeholders

Previously, primary stakeholders were defined as those that play a direct role in the value creation processes of the firm. Employees, customers, suppliers, financiers (including shareholders), and communities have been identified as primary stakeholders and have been discussed previously. *Secondary stakeholders* are not normally engaged in the value creation process; however, they still have an interest in the decisions and outcomes of the firm. For example, trade unions are charged with protecting the interests of their members. Government agencies and regulators ensure that laws are obeyed and that the well-being of citizens and the environment are protected. In addition, a variety of NGOs, religious organizations, and activists exist to support particular causes or constituencies.[6] These stakeholders are *influencers* because their actions are designed to influence firm decisions and behavior.[7] Some of the common tools secondary stakeholders use to influence firms include boycotts, legal suits, social media campaigns, strikes, walkouts, research studies, and protests.

A large firm is subject to so many competing requests from second-ary stakeholders that it is difficult to determine which ones to consider when management decisions are made. Of course, government agencies and regulators cannot be ignored, and many companies have experienced difficulties due to strikes and walkouts when the demands of trade unions are set aside. Firms tend to pay more attention to other types of second-ary stakeholders (i.e., NGOs) when they are larger, well established and widely known, part of a network or alliance with other firms with the same interests, and when their requests are deemed more legitimate in the eyes of the public.[8] For example, a group like the Environmental Defense Fund has more power because its interests are aligned with those of other environmental groups such as the Nature Conservancy, the Natural Resources Defense Council, and the Sierra Club Foundation.

Secondary stakeholders (besides government entities or trade unions) *ordinarily* don't add much value to the firm's value creation system. Consequently, the best strategy is to monitor their interests and demands and respond with concrete actions only to those that are legitimate or would seem to be legitimate in the eyes of the firm's primary stakeholders.[9] Also, sometimes it is possible to work with a secondary stakeholder to prevent problems from occurring, such as the case of a firm working with an environmental group to design a new plant that is as environmentally friendly as possible. In addition, it may even be possible to enhance a part of the value creation system through listening to the views of a secondary stakeholder.[10] For example, a firm might work with an NGO that focuses on employee rights to create a work contract that is likely to be seen favorably by both current and future employees.

Analysis of Broad Environmental Influences

In addition to the external forces already discussed, four other environmental forces can have a profound influence on the firm's value creation system and its ability to achieve its objectives. These forces originate in the economic, sociocultural, political, and technological environments. While forces in the broader environment can have a tremendous impact on a firm, individual firms typically have only a marginal ability to influence these forces. In rare cases, individual firms can influence trends in their broad environment, as when innovations at Intel or Microsoft influence technological trends in the high-tech industries. Typically, the cases in which a firm has a meaningful impact on the broad environment are the exception rather than the rule. Consequently, the emphasis in this book is primarily on analyzing and responding to these segments of the environment.

Analysis of the broad environment can help managers identify both threats and opportunities. Alternative strategies can then be devised that will help the firm respond to threats and take advantage of the opportunities, especially when combined with the other analyses described in this book. Managers should evaluate these forces at the domestic and, as appropriate, global levels.

Economic Forces

Economic forces can have a profound influence on organizational behavior and performance, either directly or through industry forces. Economics is an entire discipline by itself, and a concise book like this can do no more than provide highlights concerning traditional economic fundamentals. A more comprehensive view can be gained elsewhere. Nonetheless, this section identifies some of the most important forces every business firm should track.

As mentioned in the introduction to this section, the growth rate of the economy influences the growth rate of the industry and thus the intensity of industry competition. This is because economic growth has a large impact on consumer demand for products and services. Consequently, organizations should consider forecasts of economic growth in determining when to make critical resource allocation decisions such as plant expansions.

One of the most important forces to track is gross domestic product (GDP), a summary measure representing the output of a nation's economy. Frequently, this measure is divided by the population of a country, resulting in GDP per capita, a widely used measure of the potential buying power of a nation's citizens. Forecasting economic indicators such as GDP is important, but difficult. Business cycles exist, represented by periods of strong economic growth followed by economic downturns, but it is hard to determine precisely when the economy is going to turn or how severe each change will be.

Inflation rates can also influence a variety of business decisions and outcomes, both directly through the prices firms pay for factors of production and in terms of the interest firms have to pay. High inflation can lead to high interest, and high interest payments can constrain the strategic flexibility of firms by making new ventures and capacity expansions prohibitively expensive. Low interest rates (frequently associated with low inflation) make investment opportunities look more attractive because they are less costly to finance. In theory, the resulting increase in business investments should also help stimulate economic growth. Consequently, many governments are highly proactive in taking actions to curb inflationary forces and control interest rates.

Firms that are involved in multiple countries should track economic growth, inflation, and interest rates in all the countries in which they are present. In addition, foreign exchange rates and trade balances can be important. The precise elements to be tracked and analyzed will vary depending on factors such as the nature of the industry, the size and diversity of the firm (including international diversity), and firm dependence on economic forces. With regard to economic dependence, the question is whether the firm is in a countercyclical business, which is a business that tends to do better than other businesses during recessions.

Sociocultural Forces

Analysis of societal forces is important for a variety of reasons. One reason is that stakeholder groups are also members of society, so some of their values and beliefs are derived from broader societal influences. Consequently, firms that are serious about serving their stakeholders are in a better position to provide value to them if they understand what they find important.

Closely related to serving stakeholders, firms may also enhance their general reputations and reduce the risk of hurting their image by anticipating and adjusting for sociocultural trends. One global trend of some importance is the "green" movement. A key component of this movement, *sustainable development*, supports a pattern of economic decision making that uses resources to meet current human needs while also ensuring that adequate resources will be available for generations to come. In response to increasing public awareness of environmental issues and global warming, many large companies now publish annual sustainability reports. Movements that express distrust and discontent with capitalism and its various institutions may also have implications for corporations and other for-profit organizations at some point in the future. In this sense, such movements might be considered a threat, perhaps best addressed by reinforcing organizational values such as transparency, fairness, respect, and honesty.[11]

Societal trends may also offer business opportunities. For instance, societal interest in health and fitness has led to business opportunities in the home fitness, nutritional supplements, and low-carbohydrate food

industries. Also, demographic changes in society, such as an aging population, can stimulate growth in health maintenance and leisure industries
and some luxury products and services.

Finally, ongoing assessment of sociocultural trends can also help
businesses avoid restrictive legislation. Industries and organizations that
police themselves are less likely to be the target of legislative activity. Two
examples in the United States are the Sarbanes-Oxley Act of 2002 and the
Dodd-Frank Act of 2010. The Sarbanes-Oxley Act of 2002 was passed
by Congress in response to the accounting scandals that surfaced involving Arthur Andersen, WorldCom, Enron, and others. The act established
tighter rules in regard to executive and director securities trading, increases
executive responsibility for corporate controls and public disclosure of
financial information, and increases penalties for corporate fraud.[12] The
Dodd-Frank Act of 2010 resulted from excesses in the financial industry
that magnified the major recession that began in late 2007. It provided a
blueprint for new regulations for the U.S. financial markets and included
the establishment of a new Consumer Financial Protection Bureau.[13]
New legislation is even more common in the environmental protection
area (e.g., pollution). Because of societal concern about privacy rights and
the size and influence of Internet-based firms and technology providers,
this is an area that is ripe for additional regulation. Each new piece of
regulation brings with it new costs to businesses that are ultimately passed
on to consumers.

The economic forces discussed previously in this section often interact
with sociocultural forces. In the United States, birth rates (a sociocultural
force) are low, and because of improved health care and lifestyles (another
sociocultural force), more people are living longer. This demographic shift
toward an older population is influencing economic forces in society. For
example, the aging population means that demand for premium services
are high, but simultaneously, there are shortages of young workers to fill
the entry-level jobs in some industries, which may ultimately drive up
wage rates and lead to inflation. So, for example, a service firm tracking
these trends may project that its demand will go up as it sells its services
to the older customers, but its wage rates may increase as well, leading to
lower unit profitability.

To assess the effect of the interdependent sociocultural and economic forces, organizations often model their business environments by proposing and evaluating different scenarios.[14] *Scenario planning* based on basic trends can help managers make better decisions. Scenarios are often framed as "optimistic," "pessimistic," and "most likely" by applying different assumptions and interpretations of various economic and sociocultural trend data. Continuing with the previous example, the firm may use various demand and wage rate assumptions to build several future scenarios as a way of evaluating different business options. These scenarios can be updated as information becomes more certain and may be used for evaluating multiple courses of action, such as capacity expansions or investments in labor-saving technologies. Of course, scenario planning is not limited only to the sociocultural and economic forces. It can be used across all of a firm's environmental forces.

Political Forces

As the previous section demonstrated, sociocultural forces can influence political forces. Political forces, both at home and abroad, are significant determinants of organizational actions. Governments and other political bodies provide and enforce the rules by which organizations operate. Even in the United States, which is considered a "free" market economy, no organization is allowed the privilege of total autonomy from government regulations. Governments can encourage new business formation through tax incentives and subsidies; they can restructure organizations, as in the case of General Motors; and they can totally close organizations that do not comply with laws, ordinances, or regulations. Government intervention in business has increased in the United States and other countries in recent years, although the trend toward intervention followed a period of fairly significant decline in interventionism worldwide. Alliances and treaties among governments provide an additional level of complexity for organizations with significant foreign operations. Among the most influential are those associated with trade policies and tariffs.

The amount of time and effort organizations should devote to learning about regulations, complying with them, and fostering good relationships with regulatory agencies and their representatives depends, in part, on the industry. Some laws and regulations pertain to only one industry, such as nuclear energy (i.e., Japan Atomic Energy Agency) or banking (i.e., Federal Financial Supervisory Authority in Germany). Others cut across industry boundaries and apply more generally to all organizations, such as those promulgated by the Occupational Safety and Health Administration in the United States. In some industries, such as pharmaceuticals and military and defense contracting, organizations employ entire departments of analysts that are dedicated to studying regulations and ensuring compliance.

Technological Forces

Technological change results in new products, services, and, in some cases, entire new industries. It can also change the way society behaves and what society expects. Internet businesses, drones, satellite systems, and super-advanced smartphones are technological innovations that have experienced extraordinary growth in recent years, leaving formerly well-established industries stunned, creating new industry segments, and influencing the way many people approach work and leisure. Computers and telecommunications technologies, for example, have played an essential role in creating the increasingly global marketplace.

Technology refers to human knowledge about products and services and the way they are made and delivered. Technologies typically evolve through a series of steps, each of which has its own set of implications for managers. Inventions are new ideas or technologies that are proven to work in a laboratory. They are made every day in corporate research laboratories, universities, and by individuals. Only a handful of those inventions, however, are ever developed into viable products and services. When they are, they are often called innovations. Most technological innovations take the form of new products or processes, such as driverless cars, new apps, or advanced production technologies. A basic innovation, such as the microprocessor, the Internet, fiber optics, or mapping of the human genome, impacts much more than one type of product or service or even one industry. These are innovations that cut across the whole global economy.

To avoid being blindsided by a new technology, organizations should monitor technological developments in industries other than their own, evaluate the possible consequences for their own products and markets, and create strategies that take advantage of changes. In a historic failure of great magnitude, Kodak, at one time the international market leader in photographic products, failed to respond quickly enough to digital technology. In contrast, Canon successfully made the transition and experienced market success with its products.

To help identify trends and anticipate their timing, organizations may participate in several kinds of technological forecasting efforts. In general, organizations may monitor trends by studying research journals, government reports, and patent filings. Another more formal method of technological forecasting is to solicit the opinion of experts outside of the organization. These experts may be interviewed directly or contacted as part of a formal survey. A third method is to develop scenarios of alternative technological futures, which capture different rates of innovation and various emerging technologies. These scenarios then become part of the larger scenario-planning effort described in the previous section, allowing organizations to conduct "what-if" analyses and to develop alternative plans for responding to new innovations.

In addition to forecasting, some organizations establish strategic alliances with universities or other companies to engage in joint research and development projects, which allow the companies to keep abreast of new trends. For example, most of the established pharmaceutical firms have created partnerships with smaller, innovative biotechnology research firms in order to capture the next generation of biotech-driven product and process technologies. In some cases, alliances take the form of *open innovation*, which means that collaborators and competitors openly share knowledge and enter or exit the network as they please. Open innovation alliances are common in the cell-phone industry, where changes in technology and customer preferences require rapid innovation. With a well-thought-out plan for monitoring technological trends, an organization can better prepare itself to receive early warnings about trends and how they might result in opportunities to create more value for stakeholders or threats to the existing value creation system.

This section has demonstrated the influence of economic, sociocultural, political, and technological forces on the firm and its ability to create value for stakeholders. Consequently, firms should monitor and, to the extent possible, predict trends in these areas. This information can then be used in devising strategies for enhancing competitiveness and creating more value for stakeholders through the firm's value creation system. Table 5.1 summarizes all of the analyses described in this chapter.

Table 5.1 Summary of analysis of environmental influences

Component of the environment	Objective	Examples of analysis tools
Intensity of Competition	Evaluate the level and nature of competitive forces in an industry so firm can create strategies that offset these influences	Factors such as number of competitors, industry growth, product differentiation, entry/exit barriers, and substitutes
Power of Competitors	Determine which competitors have most potential to influence value creation system	Factors such as size, possession of valuable resources, reputation, exclusive relationships, network centrality, and political connections
Community	Assess power and determine nature of relationships with members of community and their political leaders	Power analysis based on attractiveness of location, firm growth, and other factors; nature of relationship based on factors such as tax structure, local press, social media, legal issues
Financiers	Assess power and determine nature of relationships with financial intermediaries and shareholders	Intermediary power based on factors such as industry stability, competition among financiers, and firm condition; shareholder power based on existence of large block shareholders
Secondary Stakeholders	Determine which secondary stakeholders are most salient and thus deserve more attention	Regulators and unions are automatically salient; others based on size, age, influence, links to other groups, legitimacy of interests to public
Economic Forces	Evaluate economic forces with highest potential to influence firm and its value creation system, especially with regard to growth	Track and forecast growth in GDP, inflation, interest rates, exchange rates, trade balances

Component of the environment	Objective	Examples of analysis tools
Sociocultural Forces	Evaluate sociocultural trends to understand stakeholders, enhance and protect reputation, find new business opportunities, and avoid restrictive legislation	Widely available news outlets and research reports; scenario planning that combines with economic analysis
Political Forces	Keep current on regulation and political trends; use this information in planning	Stay current on new laws and regulations that can affect the firm and its value creation system
Technological Forces	Keep current on inventions and innovations that could be useful in improving the firm's value creation system	Track trends in industry as well as other industries that may have new technologies that could be applied to the firm's value creation system; pay close attention to basic innovations that have broad potential

Summary of Findings from Strategic Analysis

As mentioned previously, the information obtained through strategic analysis has two primary objectives. First, internal resource analysis can help managers determine whether the firm has any resource-based sources of competitive advantage and whether those advantages are sustainable. The resource analysis can also contribute to the second major objective— to determine which areas of a firm's value creation system might be holding back the creation of more value within the system. Chapter 6 will examine how to use the information gained through strategic analysis to achieve these specific objectives. However, at this point it is often helpful to begin organizing the information around particular themes. One of the most common ways to do this is with what is called a SWOT analysis.[15] There are many variations on this technique, but the tried and proven method is described here.

Based primarily on internal resource analysis, a firm first identifies its strengths (S) and weaknesses (W). *Strengths* come from resources and capabilities the firm possesses that contribute significantly to the value created for stakeholders. However, it is possible that many or most competitors also possess these strengths. Consequently, it is also helpful to determine which of these are rare as well and might also be difficult or costly to imitate. This analysis is, of course, consistent with the tools provided at the beginning of Chapter 4. *Weaknesses*, on the other hand, are resources or capabilities that the firm does not possess and that could be hurting competitiveness by reducing the efficiency of the firm's value creation system. Chapter 6 will help to fine-tune this analysis; however, it is helpful to begin to identify any obvious weaknesses.

Opportunities (O) and threats (T) typically arise from what is happening in the external environment; however, they can also come from value chain participants (e.g., suppliers and customers). *Opportunities* are conditions that allow a firm to take advantage of organizational strengths, overcome organizational weaknesses, and/or neutralize environmental threats. *Threats* are conditions that could hurt firm competitiveness or the efficiency and effectiveness of its value creation system. Firm managers often consider the results from this analysis as they identify strategic alternatives and formulate strategies. The general idea is that strategies should be formulated to take advantage of internal strengths and opportunities, to overcome internal weaknesses, or to neutralize threats.

Chapters 4 and 5 have provided detailed guidelines for conducting a full strategic analysis of a firm's value creation system and the external environment in which it exists, resulting in a vast and valuable collection of strategic intelligence. Chapter 6 will explain how to assess this information to develop specific strategies.

Notes

1. M.E. Porter. 1980. *Competitive Strategy: Techniques for Analyzing Industries and Competitors* (New York, NY: The Free Press); J.S. Harrison and C.H. St. John. 2014. *Foundations in Strategic Management.* 6th ed. (Mason, OH: South-Western), Chapter 2.
2. R.E. Freeman, J.S. Harrison, and S. Zygliodopoulos. 2018. *Stakeholder Theory: Concepts and Strategies* (Cambridge, UK: Cambridge University Press), Chapter 5.
3. Freeman et al., *Stakeholder Theory*, Chapter 5.
4. This section was strongly influenced by Freeman et al., *Stakeholder Theory*, Chapter 5.

5. Freeman et al., *Stakeholder Theory*, Chapter 5.

6. W. Su and E.W.K. Tsang. 2015. "Product Diversification and Financial Performance: The Moderating Role of Secondary Stakeholders," *Academy of Management Journal* 58, 1128–48.

7. R.E. Freeman. 1984. *Strategic Management: A Stakeholder Approach* (Boston, MA: Pitman).

8. J.S. Harrison and A.C. Wicks. 2019. "Harmful Stakeholder Strategies," *Journal of Business Ethics.* doi.org/10.1007/s10551-019-04310-9; R.K. Mitchell, B.R. Agle, and D. Wood. 1997. "Toward a Theory of Stakeholder Identification and Salience: Defining the Principle of Who and What Really Counts," *Academy of Management Review* 22, pp. 853–86.

9. T. Thijssens, L. Bolllen, and H. Hassink. 2015. "Secondary Stakeholder Influence on CSR Disclosure: An Application of Stakeholder Salience Theory," *Journal of Business Ethics* 132, pp. 873–91.

10. S.L. Hart and S. Sharma. 2004. "Engaging Fringe Stakeholders for Competitive Imagination." *Academy of Management Executive* 18, no. 1, pp. 7–18.

11. J.S. Harrison, D.A. Bosse, and R.A. Phillips. 2010. "Managing for Stakeholders, Stakeholder Utility Functions, and Competitive Advantage," *Strategic Management Journal* 31, pp. 58–74.

12. Sarbanes-Oxley. https://pcaobus.org/About/History/Documents/PDFs/Sarbanes_Oxley_Act_of_2002.pdf, (accessed February 8, 2020).

13. W. Long. 2012. "Financial Regulation Is Hurting New York," *Wall Street Journal*, April 20, A1.

14. O.L. Kuye and B.E.A. Oghojafor. 2011. "Scenario Planning as a Recipe for Corporate Performance: The Nigerian Manufacturing Sector Experience," *International Journal of Business & Management* 6, no. 2, pp. 170–79; P.J.H. Schoemaker. 1995. "Scenario Planning: A Tool for Strategic Thinking," *Sloan Management Review* 36, no. 2, pp. 25–40.

15. S. Ghazinoory, M. Abdi, and M. Azadegan-Mehr. 2011. "SWOT Methodology: A State-of-the-Art Review for the Past, a Framework for the Future," *Journal of Business, Economics and Management* 12, pp. 24–48; C.W. Hofer and D. Schendel. 1978. *Strategy Formulation: Analytical Concepts* (St. Paul, MN: West Publishing Co.).

CHAPTER 6

System Assessment: Tools to Guide Strategic Decisions

The last two chapters described a variety of analysis techniques managers can use to come to an understanding of the firm's competitive situation and the efficiency and effectiveness of the firm's value creation system in providing value to stakeholders. The information collected is called strategic intelligence. *System assessment*, the topic of this chapter, uses the strategic intelligence gathered through strategic analysis to diagnose how well the value creation system is working and then address any weak areas that may be holding back the creation of more value in the system. In essence, this assessment leads to the development of strategies to overcome deficiencies. One of the important results of a system assessment is the identification of problem areas, which are parts of the system that require increased management attention and resources.

This chapter begins with an assessment of internal resources, which is based on the internal resource analysis described in Chapter 4. The resource assessment section will be followed by a description of various tools used for assessing the value chain and the stakeholders that make it work. The final section will discuss how the output of all these analyses and assessments is converted into strategies.

Assessment of Internal Resources and Capabilities

Chapter 4 provided a set of criteria for determining whether a resource or capability is a source of sustainable competitive advantage. Remember, if a resource has market value because of its ability to differentiate a product or service or produce it at lower cost, and if it is at least somewhat unique or rare, then it has the *potential* to be a source of competitive advantage.

If the organization is suited to exploiting the resource or capability and managers are both aware of and acting on it, then it is a source of competitive advantage. The advantage becomes sustainable if it is difficult or costly to imitate. If such a resource or capability exists, then the appropriate strategic response is to do all that is necessary to maintain and protect it. A simple example is that a firm with a valuable and rare technology should either patent it or, if possible, keep it a secret. Sometimes, firms intentionally avoid patents because they require detailed documentation of the technology, which conveys knowledge of it to competitors. Firms should also be very protective of their trademarks, brand names, and the company name. One way to do this is to be highly responsive to stakeholders so as to avoid negative reciprocity. As another example, if a group of employees is highly innovative or exceptionally productive, the firm could take steps to make sure they remain with the firm.

Another use of information about the positive competitive potential of a resource or capability is to find new ways to utilize them. Consider the Disney brand and how many ways it is used. Also, unique production technologies can often be used to manufacture new products. In addition, special relationships with stakeholders can be used to develop new business opportunities. As another example, a firm that owns properties in uniquely valuable locations, such as Silicon Valley or Ka'anapali Beach in Maui, can expand what they do on those properties. It is possible also to develop strategies that use these sorts of resources or capabilities to take advantage of opportunities that are identified during the analysis of the external environment.

The reality is that beyond a company name, patent, or brand name, most firms probably don't have a resource or capability that is a clear source of sustainable competitive advantage. It is simply too easy to imitate most resources and capabilities over time. In these situations, a firm may want to attempt to acquire one. One of the most popular ways for an existing firm to acquire such a resource or capability is through acquisition of a firm that already possesses one. Indeed, such acquisitions are very common in the biotechnology and high-tech industries, among others. Of course, firms also conduct their own R&D and marketing research in an effort to develop technologies, products, and services that are uniquely valuable.

As mentioned previously, although it is fairly easy to imitate most resources and capabilities, it is much harder for competitors to imitate an internal group or system that is able to produce innovation on a continuing basis. Consequently, a focus on developing strong internal innovation systems may actually be more fruitful than focusing on any one new product or service. A firm might also try to develop a special or exclusive arrangement with a stakeholder such as a supplier that sells a unique product or service.

Internal resource analysis also includes financial resources, employees and managers, and the firm's governance structure. A number of financial and operating metrics should be included, as well as some general characteristics that should be evaluated, such as the structure of the board (e.g., independence) and whether there is evidence of agency problems (see Tables 4.1 and 4.2). Managers should track trends and make essential comparisons with direct competitors in these areas to the extent possible.

Competitive benchmarking involves direct competitor-to-competitor comparisons of products, services, processes, resources, and performance outcomes. This sort of process gained popularity a few decades ago. However, some strategists criticized the method because bringing a firm up to the level of a rival or an industry standard is never going to lead to a competitive advantage. The logic seems convincing. After all, bringing the quality or serviceability of a product up to the same level as a competitor is not likely to impress customers or lead them to want to purchase one firm's product over another. From a purely resource-based perspective, this is accurate. Nonetheless, the logic does not hold for a systems perspective.

From a systems perspective, a weak resource or missing capability could be holding back the creation of value in the entire system. For example, disgruntled or inadequately trained employees are likely to negatively influence the firm's productivity, innovation, and, ultimately, its financial performance and the reputation of its products. Poorly managed or inadequate finances can limit the ability of the firm to make investments across all of the other resource areas. A weak brand can limit the firm's ability to attract customers as well as high-quality employees. Agency problems can reduce the ability of a firm to raise capital by depressing earnings, dividends, and the share price.

Benchmarking can help to assess whether there are problems in any of the resource areas or even in the firm's value chain. It is one of the most powerful tools in determining which parts of the value creation system require more attention and resources. As these problem areas are addressed, the firm becomes more competitive. Competitive advantage, from a systems perspective, comes not from any one valuable resource or capability but from a superior value creation system. Remember that even if the firm does possess resources or capabilities that provide competitive advantage, it can still improve the amount of value created for stakeholders by improving its value creation system.

Assessment of the Value Chain

Although there are a number of aspects of the firm's value chain that are worthy of assessment, efficiency and innovation are the two most fundamental. Efficiency and innovation are important in every part of the chain. They are also closely related, as technological innovation can lead to efficiency in the value chain.

Assessing Efficiency

Chapter 4 provided a number of analysis tools that are useful in assessing each area of the value chain (see Tables 4.1 and 4.2). Many of these tools are indicators of efficiency. Relevant financial ratios include labor force efficiency, asset turnover, inventory turnover, and gross profit margin. Consultants and third-party research firms can also be helpful at times in determining where there may be efficiency problems. These are just examples. Many other possibilities exist, depending on the needs of a specific business and the nature of its value chain. As was the case with resource assessment, benchmarking can be very effective in finding those areas of the value chain that are holding back the creation of additional value. Sometimes, these problem areas are obvious, whereas at other times they are not. When it is not obvious, on the basis of value chain analysis, which part of the value chain is holding back creation of additional value in the system, other tools may be necessary.

Another practical way to identify weaknesses in the value chain is to determine which areas have no slack.[1] *Organizational slack* is the unused capacity a firm maintains in one or more areas of its value chain or in the value creation system as a whole. From a financial perspective, it could mean that a firm has excess cash or untapped borrowing capacity owing to very low leverage. Financial slack can help a firm endure recessions or adapt to changes in its environment, but too much slack is a sign of inefficiency.

The same principles that apply to financial slack can be applied to other basic and support areas of a firm's value chain. The key is to identify where the organization does not have a healthy amount of slack—whether it is too much or too little. For example, if managers or employees are overworked in a particular area, perhaps leading to burnout, increased illness, or turnover, it could mean that there is no slack. In addition to monitoring these negative employee effects, employee surveys and focus groups are also an effective way to assess slack (or its absence). Ordinarily, employees will share this sort of information when they are asked.

In terms of operations, the area with no slack is the area that is running out of resources. For example, if it is difficult to obtain needed supplies on time, it could be an indication that there is no slack with regard to incoming supplies. If communications with customers are insufficient, it could be an indication that the marketing management area has no slack. If customers are getting their orders late, it could be a result of a lack of slack in the distribution area. Contractual problems, legal issues, or fines could be an indication that there are an insufficient number of legal experts—that the legal support area has no slack. Lack of innovation in any part of a firm's value chain could be an indication that knowledge and learning systems have no slack.

Because a firm's IT system is critical to managing the entire value chain, it requires special attention during the assessment process. A measure such as the total cost of IT as a percentage of cost-of-goods-sold, total administrative cost, or sales can provide one indication of the efficiency of the system, but perhaps more important is an assessment of its effectiveness. One of the best indicators of an effective IT system is whether managers and employees have the information they need when they need it. If decisions are delayed or are not as good as they could be if better information were provided to decision makers, it could be a sign that the IT system needs improvement. It then becomes one of the problem areas that require additional management attention and resources.

Assessing Innovation

Product and process innovation are both critical to a firm. If a firm's products and services are losing some of their desirability, leading to declining sales, then product innovation processes or the people responsible for them may be the problem. If production efficiency is declining or even remaining the same, then process innovation may be what is holding up the creation of additional value. A ratio such as R&D intensity, especially when compared with that of competitors, is a useful tool for determining whether the firm is allocating enough resources to innovation. Some of the efficiency ratios, such as labor force efficiency or growth in sales, can also help. Customer surveys and focus groups are among the best means to assess the innovative aspects of products and services.

Although ratios, surveys, and focus groups are helpful, a firm should also assess internal factors to determine whether it is getting what it should in the area of innovation. Firms with lots of innovation have a strategic direction, culture, and leaders that encourage creativity, learning, and risk taking. Steve Jobs, the legendary past CEO of Apple, was a master at inspiring innovation in his company. He believed in the power of vision and in changing the world. He would challenge managers, researchers, and employees to dream bigger and to sell those dreams to customers. Jobs also taught that one of the keys to creativity is to connect seemingly unrelated ideas, questions, or problems from different fields.[2] Jobs' leadership kept Apple on the cutting edge of technological innovation. Table 6.1 contains a list of factors that encourage or discourage innovation. Assessment of these factors can help a firm discover what might be holding back innovation in its value creation system.

Innovative firms learn not only from their own internal R&D processes, but also from external stakeholders such as customers, suppliers, and venture partners.[3] They can learn through communications and transactions with them, and they can pursue new collaborations with them.

Table 6.1 Encouraging innovation

Focal area	Encourage innovation	Discourage innovation
Strategic direction	Strong innovation theme	Emphasis on financial returns
Organizational culture	Encourages creative thinking and risk taking	Rewards conformance and discourages novel ideas
Top management	Support innovation through resource allocations and example	Behavior encourages maintaining status quo
Communications	Open communications between and across levels	Closed-door offices and ineffective IT system
Priority given to employees	Value the ideas of all employees	Focus on researchers or managers
Rewards systems	Large rewards for internal entrepreneurs who create new value for the firm	Harsh penalties for failures such as demotions or termination
Leadership	Teamwork and collaboration	Authoritarian
Hierarchy	Flat, with decentralized decision making	Tall (many levels), with lots of bureaucracy
Resource allocations for innovation	Organizational champions who generate new ideas and gather resources to exploit them	Difficult approval process and stingy resource allocations
Internal focus	Emphasis on learning	Emphasis on measurable outcomes
Financial slack	Slack resources available to invest in promising opportunities	Tight finances (high debt, few liquid assets)

Collaborations associated with the open innovation approach mentioned previously can lead to "the pursuit of innovations across firm boundaries through the sharing of ideas, knowledge, expertise and opportunities.[4] They can help smaller firms acquire the resources they need to pursue opportunities or help larger firms overcome the challenges they face in exploring new opportunities.

Addressing Problem Areas

Once problem areas are identified, managers will want to determine ways to improve them.[5] Solutions to problems in those areas may be rather obvious, or more analysis may be required. The objective is to make changes in the firm that result in improvements to the area in the value chain that could be holding back the creation of more value in the entire system.

Force field analysis is a decision-making tool that can help facilitate organizational changes that are both predictable and desirable.[6] Having determined a problem area in the value chain that needs improvement, managers then determine which forces have the potential to move that area of the value chain in a positive direction and which forces might be holding it back (see Figure 6.1). For example, assume that productivity is lower than it should be in one part of the firm's value chain. Some of the forces that could move that area toward higher productivity could include additional training, an improved incentive system, or use of better technologies. Standing in the way could be outdated equipment, a plant that is too small, or inadequate staffing. Managers would identify these elements and then decide which of the positive forces to work on or which of the negative forces to eliminate or improve. This should result in positive movement toward the desired end state, in this case higher productivity.

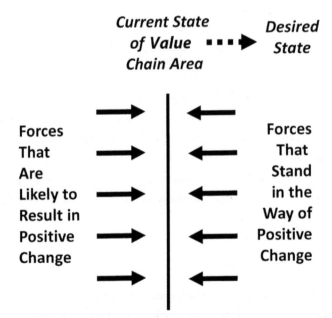

Figure 6.1 Force field analysis applied to value chain

There is, however, more to organizational change than just increasing positive forces or reducing negative forces. Firms in their current state are resistant to change.[7] Beyond the reality that most humans are resistant to the uncertainties associated with change, there are institutional factors such as organizational routines, rules, a reporting structure, various information and other systems, and a culture that define how things are done. The organization is essentially frozen. If a firm is going to change a part of its value creation system in a fundamental way, it needs to be unfrozen to some extent, at least with regard to those organizational factors that will have to change if the effort is going to be a success. A crisis is a good way to shake up an organization. A crisis could be precipitated by something as awful as a natural disaster or as routine as the entrance of a new competitor or a new, highly innovative product. A decline in operating revenues or profits could also present a crisis, as could negative press about an event that damages a firm's reputation such as a product recall, environmental fine, large legal suit, or a highly visible complaint from a stakeholder.

If a crisis does not present itself (which is, of course, a good thing), managers can still unfreeze an organization through actions such as personnel transfers, restructuring the organization chart, or pursuing a new strategy. The amount of unfreezing necessary is contingent on the size of the change. For example, a minor change might be possible through simple rule changes or reassignment of duties, whereas a major organizational change may require a more extreme shake-up. Once an organization is unfrozen, there is an opportunity to make changes, and these changes should be followed by a reinstitutionalization of routines, rules, structure, systems, and culture consistent with the changes that were made. After a change is made, there should also be follow-up to ensure that the change is producing the desired results. Chapter 7 discusses the processes for this sort of follow-up.

Assessing Stakeholders

Stakeholder assessment is another tool for determining problem areas that could be holding back value creation in the firm's value creation system.

Remember that each aspect of a firm's value creation system, including every part of its value chain, is linked to particular stakeholders (see Figure 2.3). For example, physical resources and production systems are linked to materials and technology providers, local communities, and often product wholesalers and distributors. Financial resources are linked to customers, bondholders, shareholders, rating agencies, and a variety of financial institutions. One way to determine whether there is a problem in some part of a firm's value creation system is to assess the strength and nature of relationships with a firm's stakeholders. If there is a problem with one of these relationships, then it is probable that the area to which they are connected is holding back that part of the system. Reciprocity will be at a reduced level, leading to less information sharing, resource sharing, cooperation, motivation, and loyalty. Consequently, those stakeholders may require a larger allotment of management attention and resources to repair the relationships.

Table 1.1 in Chapter 1 provided a large number of measures of what might be called "stakeholder performance," which is firm performance from the perspective of each primary stakeholder. Many of these measures were incorporated into the strategic analysis and system assessment tools found in Chapters 4 and 5. All of these indicators are useful in determining which stakeholder relationships might need repair in order to unlock additional value creation. However, another effective way to determine which stakeholders need more attention is to assess their power in combination with their strategic importance.

Stakeholder Power and Strategic Importance

Chapters 4 and 5 provided tools for determining the economic power of primary stakeholders, including employees, customers, suppliers, financiers, and communities. Powerful stakeholders are already likely to attract the attention of managers. Essentially, it is unlikely that they will be neglected during strategic planning because of their power. However, what about less powerful stakeholders? Will they typically be neglected? One way to determine whether a particular stakeholder group is likely to be neglected and thus whether that stakeholder needs more attention is to compare their power with their strategic importance.[8]

Stakeholders that are crucial to the competitiveness of a firm are *strategically important*. Often, these stakeholders also possess power, but not always. For example, some employees may not be economically powerful because there is an abundance of workers who possess the same skills; however, they may still be strategically important because the quality of their work is a primary source of differentiation for the firm's products. Similarly, many suppliers may provide a particular raw material to the firm, which reduces their power; however, in some cases the timeliness of delivery or the quality of the raw material may be essential to the success of the firm's value chain.

The highest priority stakeholders are those that have both power and strategic importance; however, the stakeholders that are most likely to be neglected (and thus may need more attention) are the stakeholders with low power and high strategic importance. Because of their strategic importance, a firm may be able to enhance the value creating potential of its entire system by devoting more attention and resources to them. In addition, stakeholders with high power and low strategic importance could actually be receiving too many resources and too much management attention. In these cases, attention and resources could be reduced without damaging value creation within the firm.

The potential for overallocation of resources and attention to some stakeholders raises another important question. How can managers determine how many resources and how much attention to allocate? Two forms of justice, discussed in Chapter 2, are relevant here: distributional justice can be applied to the question of resource allocations, and procedural justice pertains to the attention paid to stakeholders.

Remember that distributional justice means that stakeholders are receiving a fair reward for their contributions to the value creation processes of the firm. For example, an employee is receiving fair compensation and benefits or customers are getting good value for the price they pay. If resource distributions to a stakeholder are not fair, then their motivation levels will decrease, and they are likely to terminate their business with the firm if it is reasonable to do so (e.g., contract has come to an end or it is easy to find new employment). If distributions are too high, it is likely that the firm will not have enough resources to allocate to other essential areas of the value chain, resulting in financial stress. Also, some stakeholders are likely to resent that another stakeholder is being given special treatment. This resentment can alter their behavior toward the firm.

The optimal allocation of value is dependent on each stakeholder's *opportunity cost*, which is what they would receive from engaging in the same sort of activity with another firm. To unlock the benefits that come from reciprocity, a firm should allocate a level of value that is just noticeably above a stakeholder's opportunity cost. For an employee, this would be compensation that is just noticeably above what they would receive for doing the same work for another employer. For a customer, this would be receiving a product or service that is a just noticeably better value (quality/price) than what they would receive from another firm.

Procedural justice is highly relevant to determining how much attention a firm should pay to various stakeholders. Based on the description found in Chapter 2, procedural justice means that a stakeholder believes that their needs and opinions have been accounted for in the decisions the firm makes, even if they are not exactly the decisions they would like the firm to make. This pertains, of course, to decisions that affect them. From the stakeholder's perspective, they will feel unjustly dealt with if they do not receive the amount of attention they would receive from another firm making the same sort of decision. On the other hand, if the decision processes of a firm are too complex to handle efficiently and productivity is reduced as a result, then it is probable that there are too many stakeholders involved in decisions or too much input has been requested. The optimal level of attention to stakeholders during decisions that may affect them is achieved when they feel that the decision process has been fair and when no particular stakeholder is given what is perceived as an unjustifiably higher level of attention.

Managing Powerful Stakeholders

As discussed in previous chapters, powerful stakeholders often possess scarce or differentiated resources that the firm requires for its value chain work effectively. They may also possess political power or be central in a business network that is important to the firm. Stakeholders with a lot of power influence the amount of environmental uncertainty facing the firm. For example, Toyota and Walmart both have a large influence on the uncertainty many of their suppliers experience owing to the large orders they make. Losing their account could spell disaster. Similarly, a powerful technology supplier or financier can influence the uncertainty faced by a producer. Of course, there are other uncertainties coming from broad environmental forces such as the economy, but a firm can't have much influence on those types of influences. Typically, the best strategy is to adapt to broader environmental forces over which the firm has little control. On the other hand, uncertainty coming from powerful stakeholders is easier to address.

One of the most effective ways to deal with a powerful stakeholder is to make them a stronger partner in value creation through *cooperative strategies*. As firms cooperate with powerful stakeholders, their fortunes become intertwined.[9] This provides an element of predictability and an ability to jointly create value or achieve objectives that are important to both the firm and its stakeholders. Cooperative strategies can also help a firm deal with increasing global interconnectedness, rapid technological innovation, and the increasing competitiveness of the world economy. Of course, these strategies can also be highly profitable. In general, stakeholders that are the highest priority for cooperative relationships are those that have the strongest influence on the outcomes of the organization.

Cooperative strategies come in many forms, although many of them can be classified as strategic alliances. A *strategic alliance* is any kind of cooperative strategy in which firms combine resources and capabilities to pursue common objectives. A *joint venture* is a type of strategic alliance in which two or more firms come together to form a legally independent company.[10] This might also be called an equity strategic alliance. Nonequity strategic alliances can take a variety of forms. They are often established through long-term contracts. A long-term contract (as opposed to a shorter one) aligns the interests of a firm with powerful stakeholders because they understand that their performance and outcomes are more than just temporarily intertwined. Both equity and nonequity strategic alliances can be formed to pursue objectives such as developing new products, entering new markets, reducing manufacturing or distribution costs, joint promotion of products and services, dealing with forces in the external environment, or reducing competition by forming exclusive arrangements that make it harder for other firms to compete.

Cooperative strategies do not need to involve equity or contractual partnerships with stakeholders. There are many other ways to turn powerful stakeholders into powerful allies. One common technique is to appoint a representative from an important stakeholder firm to the board of directors. For example, the CEO or board member of a supplier firm may sit on the firm's board. An interlocking directorate occurs anytime the same individual sits on multiple boards. This is an effective way to align the interests of multiple firms, provide increased communication and advice, and establish a gateway for other types of alliances.

Another strategy that aligns the interests of firms with their stakeholders is to invite them to participate in research and development projects or to provide input into important organizational decisions. Organizations are also creating more linkages through online collaborations and joint communications systems. Cooperative strategies that involve multiple stakeholders also include trade groups, associations, research consortia, and alliance networks. *Alliance networks* are groups of autonomous firms that cooperate with each other because of mutual interests.[11] These networks are often organized around a strategic center or "hub firm," which is a prominent firm that coordinates cooperative activities among network members and facilitates transfer of valuable information.

To combat collapsing product and process life cycles and to get a jump on new emerging technologies, competitors are also joining forces in increasing numbers. Although cooperation in price-setting, called collusion, is illegal in the United States and many other countries, rival organizations may still form partnerships for technological advancement, for new product development, to enter new or foreign markets, or to influence government regulation through lobbying or other political tactics.[12]

Nonmarket Strategies

A firm's nonmarket environment includes relationships and interactions with government leaders and regulators, nongovernmental organizations (NGOs), and activists. You will recognize that these latter stakeholders were previously identified among a firm's secondary stakeholders. Some people would put communities in this group because they impose similar constraints on the firm and can, under some circumstances, be a threat to the achievement of the firm's objectives. However, there is more of a mutually dependent relationship between a firm and the communities in which they operate, so they are treated as primary stakeholders in this book.

Chapter 5 discussed what makes certain nonmarket stakeholders powerful and also suggested ways to turn them into a positive force for value creation by including them or their ideas in the decision processes of a firm. Although this is one way to handle powerful nonmarket stakeholders, firms sometimes use what are called nonmarket strategies to tip the balance of power with governments, NGOs, and activists. Nonmarket strategies are patterns of action taken by a firm in an effort to make its institutional and societal environment more conducive to achieving its objectives.[13] These strategies vary widely, but there are two common approaches. The first is to influence public opinion, and the second is to influence the "rules of the game."

The first basic approach to nonmarket strategies works from the idea that a firm's relationships and market interactions with stakeholders are influenced by public opinions about a firm, which are captured in its reputation. Sometimes, society at large views a firm in a negative light because of the business in which it engages. For example, a large part of society looks unfavorably on the petroleum and forestry industries because they harm the environment. A similar view exists regarding the tobacco and alcohol industries because their products harm people. These attitudes can influence demand directly, because customers make purchase decisions, in part, on the basis of their attitudes toward particular firms and industries. In addition to the direct impact this sort of negative attitude has on sales, it can also influence government regulation in countries in which political leaders are elected by the public.

Firms in industries with bad reputations have used a variety of strategies to address this problem. They have gone directly to the community through public relations media campaigns to present their business in a positive light (e.g., creating jobs, contributing to the economy, minimizing negative influences). In addition, they frequently engage in corporate social responsibility (CSR) initiatives through donations to charities or NGOs, volunteer programs, CSR reporting, or by supporting work policies that are favorable to particular groups, such as minorities, released felons, or people with special needs. As mentioned previously, they may also work directly with the nonmarket stakeholder that represents a particular cause. Of course, these types of nonmarket actions are also applicable to firms that are not in unattractive industries as a way to further enhance their reputations, along with all the associated benefits of doing so.

A second approach to nonmarket strategies generally results when government regulation is reducing the ability of a firm to succeed in achieving its objectives. In addition to hiring their own lobbyists, firms often combine with other firms, even competitors, to lobby government leaders to alter the "rules of the game," which are the laws and regulations that relate to the firm and its activities. They also make large donations to politicians, political parties, or trade organizations that represent their interests. As suggested previously, public relations efforts may also be used to sway public opinion, and as public opinion shifts, the regulatory environment can too.

There is also a darker side to nonmarket strategies in which firms use them to gain what many would consider unfair advantages over particular stakeholders. These are situations in which a firm mistreats stakeholders but, through nonmarket strategies, prevents them from reciprocating negatively toward the firm. Three historical examples help illustrate this phenomenon.[14] Amazon lobbied legislators in the state of Washington to make noncompete clauses enforceable for many of its workers. In a second example, after the Natural Resources Defense Council claimed that a particular chemical used in apple orchards was harmful to people, apple sales declined. In response, agriculture firms and industry groups persuaded several states to pass legislation restricting speech that disparages agricultural practices. Related to this situation are what are called "Ag Gag" laws that make it illegal to conduct undercover investigations in agricultural firms. Finally, regulatory barriers tipped the power balance between automobile manufacturers and dealers by requiring that new automobiles be sold only through franchised dealers.

Strategy Creation

This chapter has outlined the process for a firm to conduct an analysis and assessment of internal resources and capabilities, which will lead to conclusions about which resources and capabilities should be carefully protected and how they might be used to create more value in the firm's value creation system. The firm can utilize competitive benchmarking based on competitor-to-competitor comparisons to identify areas in the system that are relatively weak and require more management attention and resources. Assessment of the value chain, especially with regard to efficiency and innovation, can also provide information about problem areas within the firm. It is also helpful to identify areas of the value chain with no slack.

Having determined the weaknesses in the value creation system, the firm may use force field analysis to assess what might be done to improve these problem areas. The firm may also assess stakeholders on the basis of their power and their strategic importance in order to determine which stakeholders, owing to inadequate attention or because of their great power, could be holding back the creation of more value. Ideas for addressing these issues were provided in this chapter. In addition, the broad environmental analysis described in Chapter 5 provided ideas regarding opportunities the firm might pursue to create more value for stakeholders as well as threats to be addressed before they reduce the firm's ability to create value.

It is highly likely that strategic analysis and system assessment will result in too many "good things to do" with a limited amount of resources. A firm can reallocate resources away from an area with too much slack and toward an area that needs more attention and resources, but this is probably not enough to satisfy all of the demands. Over time, a more efficient and effective value creation system will generate more revenues that can be used to continually improve the system. But since the firm is not going to do everything at once, it is necessary to establish priorities leading to a determination of what the firm will do now and what will be done later (or not at all).

It is first helpful to list all of the useful ideas that were uncovered through strategic analysis and system assessment. These are called *strategic alternatives*. These alternatives should first be screened against a firm's strategic direction—mission, vision, values, and business model. The firm should reject any alternatives that are not consistent with the first three. However, if an alternative would require a change in the business model (i.e., new target market, new asset application, change in growth strategy), it should not be rejected, but it should be noted that business model changes tend to be more difficult to carry out than alternatives that simply fine-tune the existing model.

Some strategic alternatives can be eliminated because they obviously will not be executed in the foreseeable future. This elimination may be because the alternatives are too expensive given existing resources or the ability of the firm to generate sufficient resources, are likely to destroy a lot of stakeholder value, are likely to be resisted by one or more stakeholders to the point that they will likely fail, or for some other reason determined by the managers conducting the evaluation process. It is, however, important not to eliminate an alternative just because it defies the status quo. Many good strategies do exactly that.

Some of the easy or inexpensive alternatives can be selected immediately for execution. These might be minor changes to human resources policies, fine-tuning adjustments to the way a product is marketed, inexpensive purchases of technology or equipment, hiring of one person to satisfy a need, a change of approach to the way a firm manages some aspect of external communications, or changes to the way one or more stakeholders are treated. This list of actions to pursue immediately could also include changes to the governance structure such as appointments of directors who can increase the independence or effectiveness of the board.

Now that the list of strategic alternatives is shorter, it should be easier to organize and evaluate. A number of criteria should be considered when determining which ones to implement:

1. Does the strategic alternative address an area in the firm's value creation system that is most likely to be holding back the creation of value in the whole system? The analysis and assessment processes identified which problem area or areas should have the highest priority.

2. Which alternatives address an important stakeholder relationship, where neglect of a primary stakeholder with high strategic importance and low power or a less-than-favorable relationship with a powerful stakeholder could be holding back the creation of more value?

3. Which alternatives exploit a valuable, rare, and inimitable resource or capability the firm already possesses?

4. What will be the impact of the alternative on each of a firm's primary stakeholders: customers, suppliers, employees, financiers (including shareholders), and the communities in which the firm operates?

5. What resources will the alternative require now and in the future (management, labor, skills and technology, money, equipment, land and building space, IT, etc.)?

6. How well does the alternative fit with the current culture, operations, and business model of the firm?

7. To what extent will the alternative increase or decrease financial and business risk?

8. A net present value (NPV) analysis can be helpful in this analysis for larger projects if it is possible to make reasonable estimates of expenses and revenues over time.

The exact criteria used will depend on the priorities of the firm and the values of particular decision makers.

A payoff matrix may also be helpful as a way to "keep score" so that particular alternatives can be compared against each other. Not every strategic alternative will fit well on a payoff matrix. This sort of tool is particularly helpful when used to compare a group of highly impactful strategic alternatives and when only one can be selected because of limited resources. For example, a firm in a mature industry may be trying to decide what to do to substantially increase growth in sales. Through strategic analysis, managers are able to identify four strategic alternatives that seem to be reasonable and address the problem; however, they are quite different from one another. Should the firm expand into a completely new market with an existing product, engage in a new R&D program to develop a next generation product, establish a joint venture with a firm in another country to open a new international market for all of its products, or acquire a competitor that has a product that would fit well into the firm's product portfolio? A payoff matrix can be helpful in making this decision because each of these alternatives is evaluated on the same set of criteria (see Figure 6.2).

| | CRITERIA (WEIGHTS) | | | | | |
	Growth Potential (.3)	Initial Investment (.3)	Annual Costs (.1)	Fit Within Firm (.1)	Risk Factors (.2)	TOTAL
Enter new market with existing product	3 × 0.3 = 0.9	5 × 0.3 = 1.5	3 × 0.1 = 0.3	5 × 0.1 = 0.5	3 × 0.2 = 0.6	3.8
R&D to develop next generation product	3 × 0.3 = 0.9	3 × 0.3 = 0.9	1 × 0.1 = 0.1	5 × 0.1 = 0.5	3 × 0.2 = 0.6	3.0
Joint venture to open new international market	4 × 0.3 = 1.2	3 × 0.3 = 0.9	5 × 0.1 = 0.5	5 × 0.1 = 0.5	5 × 0.2 = 1	4.1
Acquire new product via company acquisition	5 × 0.3 = 1.5	1 × 0.3 = 0.3	4 × 0.1 = 0.4	2 × 0.1 = 0.2	1 × 0.2 = 0.2	2.6

Scale: 5=excellent, 4=good, 3=fair, 2=poor, 1=very poor

Figure 6.2 Weighted payoff matrix

Criteria weights have been added to the example in Figure 6.2. They reflect the amount of value decision makers give each of the criteria. They are optional, of course, but can sometimes be helpful if alternatives are close. The sum of the weights has to equal 1. It should also be noted that the figure is oversimplified in that it includes only five criteria rather than a full list of factors that decision makers determine are important. The figure is merely an illustration of how a payoff matrix works. Another important point about a payoff matrix is that it should not be given too much weight in the decision; that is, the totals should not, by themselves, determine what the firm will do. Essentially, the matrix is a tool to help managers establish priorities regarding what is important and to enhance discussions about how the strategic alternatives are likely to impact the value creation system of the firm and its stakeholders.

Chapters 4 to 6 have discussed how to develop strategies that will help a firm improve its value creation system and facilitate achievement of its strategic direction. These strategies are translated into strategic initiatives. The next step is to develop an implementation plan and a strategic control system to make sure that the strategic initiatives are carried out.

Notes

1. A.J. Wefald, J.P. Katz, R.G. Downey, and K.G. Rust. 2010. "Organizational Slack, Firm Performance and the Role of Industry," *Journal of Managerial Issues* 22, no. 1, pp. 70–87; L.J. Bourgeois. 1981. "On the Measurement of Organizational Slack," *Academy of Management Review* 6, pp. 29–39.
2. C. Gallo. 2010. *The Innovation Secrets of Steve Jobs: Insanely Different Principles for Breakthrough Success* (New York, NY: McGraw-Hill).
3. J.S. Harrison, D.A. Bosse, and R.A. Phillips. 2010. "Managing for Stakeholders, Stakeholder Utility Functions and Competitive Advantage," *Strategic Management Journal* 31, pp. 58–74.
4. D.J. Ketchen, R.D. Ireland, and C.C. Snow. 2007. "Strategic Entrepreneurship, Collaborative Innovation, and Wealth Creation," *Strategic Entrepreneurship Journal* 1, p. 371.
5. This subsection was adapted from J.S. Harrison and S.M. Thompson. 2015. *Strategic Management of Healthcare Organizations* (New York, NY: Business Expert Press), Chapter 7.
6. K. Lewin. 1951. *Field Theory in Social Science* (New York, NY: Harper and Row); D.J. Swanson and A.S. Creed. 2014. "Sharpening the Focus of Force Field Analysis," *Journal of Change Management* 14, pp. 28–47.
7. S. Kaplan and R. Henderson. 2005. "Inertia and Incentives: Bridging Organizational Economics and Organizational Theory," *Organization Science* 16, pp. 509–21.
8. This discussion is based on J.S. Harrison and D.A. Bosse. 2013. "How Much Is Too Much? The Limits to Generous Treatment of Stakeholders," *Business Horizons* 56, pp. 313–22.
9. J.S. Harrison and C.H. St. John, "Managing and Partnering with External Stakeholders," *Academy of Management Executive* 10, no. 2, pp. 50–60.
10. M.V.S. Kumar, "Are Joint Ventures Positive Sum Games? The Relative Effects of Cooperative and Noncooperative Behavior," *Strategic Management Journal* 32, pp. 32–54.
11. A. Zaheer, R. Gozubuyuk, and H. Milanov. 2010. "It's the Connections: The Network Perspective in Interorganizational Research," *Academy of Management Perspectives* 24, no. 1, pp. 62–77; C. Dhanaraj and A. Parkhe. 2006. "Orchestrating Innovation Networks," *Academy of Management Review* 31, pp. 659–69.
12. B.R. Barringer and J.S. Harrison. 2000. "Walking a Tightrope: Creating Value through Interorganizational Relationships," *Journal of Management* 26, pp. 367–403.

13. T. Sutton and D. Bosse. 2019. "Shareholder Value Creation, Constrained Stakeholder Reciprocity, and Nonmarket Strategy." Presented at
the Academy of Management Annual Meeting, Boston; K. Mellahi, J.G.
Frynas, P. Sun and D. Siegel. 2016. "A Review of the Nonmarket Strategy
Literature: Toward a Multi-theoretic Integration," *Journal of Management*
42, pp. 143–73.

14. Sutton and Bosse, "Shareholder Value Creation."

CHAPTER 7

Implementation Planning, Strategic Control, and Organizational Structure

Most larger firms put significant time and effort into their strategic planning processes, resulting in the identification of strategies and specific initiatives to carry them out. They also tend to be good at developing detailed implementation plans for these initiatives. However, they may struggle to fully implement their plans. This is often a result of inadequate strategic controls. Unexpected events or new pressures distract managers (just the ordinary pressures of running a business are substantial), and they put new initiatives aside, expecting to come back to them. But they never make it back, and then a new strategic planning cycle comes around. Good strategic controls dramatically increase the odds that managers will follow through with the various initiatives of the strategic plan.

A *strategic control system* is "a system to support managers in assessing the relevance of the organization's strategy to its progress in the accomplishment of its goals, and when discrepancies exist, to support areas needing attention."[1] This chapter discusses the creation of implementation plans within the context of a strategic control system. This approach fits well with the systems perspective because it assumes that the control system is an integrated part of the firm's value creation system instead of a separate system that is added on after an implementation plan is developed. They should be inseparable. Given this approach, strategic control systems will be discussed first, and then detailed implementation planning will be included as part of the control system. In addition, the chapter ends with a discussion of the organization structure that ties together various components of a firm's value creation system.

Strategic Control Systems

The strategic analysis and system assessment processes will result in many initiatives, covering a wide range of organizational activities. How does a firm make sure new strategic initiatives are accomplished? A wise and widely known adage states that what gets measured gets done. The managers who establish a new strategic initiative as part of the strategic planning process often set objectives for the initiative. This is because the initiatives were selected by these managers to address particular problem areas in the value creation system, improve the relationship with a particular stakeholder, reduce the value-destroying potential of a threat emanating from the external environment, or exploit a particular opportunity. Also, these managers have a better understanding of how an initiative fits with other new and existing strategies as well as the firm's strategic direction. The objectives they set will be more effective if they have the following characteristics:

1. They are *high enough to be motivating* so that they inspire people to a higher level of performance.
2. They are *reasonable*. Otherwise people will pretty much ignore them.
3. They deal with *specific* areas of the firm that are affected most by the initiative.
4. They *can be measured*. Measurable objectives tend to be numerical, but they do not have to be. For example, objectives may be binary (it was done or it wasn't) or based on a summation of opinions of various stakeholders (through focus groups, interviews, or other contacts).
5. They are *widely understood* by all those involved in the initiative. This helps them to stay focused on meeting the objectives.
6. They are set through *participative processes*. These processes should involve some combination of the people who helped establish the initiative, other firm members who will be most involved in carrying it out, and especially the person who ultimately will be assigned with the responsibility for making sure each initiative is implemented.
7. They cover a *specific time frame* for accomplishment.[2]

Setting effective objectives around new initiatives is one part of the puzzle, but good strategic controls are based on other essential factors as well. As depicted in Figure 7.1, responsibility should be assigned to

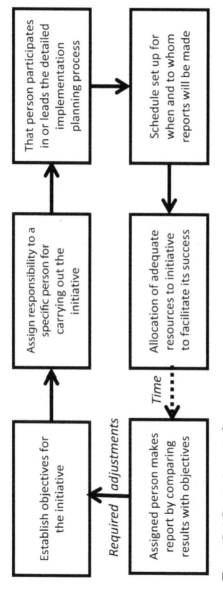

Figure 7.1 Strategic control system

specific individuals to make sure the new initiative is accomplished. The individual responsible for carrying out the initiative should be a major participant or, even better, the leader of the implementation planning process. This ensures that they understand what needs to happen and gives them greater motivation to carry out the initiative because it gives them greater "ownership." In addition, a schedule should be set for the individual to provide reports on the success of the initiative (and specifying to whom they will report). Also, adequate resources should be allocated to support the initiative.

After the set amount of time has passed, the individual with primary responsibility for carrying out the initiative returns and reports progress based on the objectives that were set. If actions and outcomes are not proceeding as planned, management must determine why and what actions should be taken to get back on course. They may determine, for example, that additional resources are needed, the schedule is too aggressive, or the underlying assumptions that were used to frame the action plan have changed. If management determines that the assumptions have changed, a significant adjustment in the action plan may be required. This is a very common occurrence when a firm is making plans to launch a new product, move into a new market, or open a new facility. Actions of competitors, changes in interest rates, and construction delays are just a few examples of the kinds of uncertainties that can provoke a repositioning of objectives and action plans.

Because this type of control system involves setting objectives and then measuring success against them, it is what is called a *feedback control system*. This type of system performs several important functions in organizations.[3] First, creating specific objectives ensures that managers at various levels and areas in the organization understand the plans and strategies that guide organizational decisions. Second, it motivates managers to stay focused on organizational interests because they know they will be held accountable for the results of their actions. Finally, this sort of system helps managers decide when to intervene in organizational processes by identifying areas requiring additional attention.

Detailed Implementation Planning

A detailed implementation plan is at the heart of a good strategic control system.[4] As mentioned previously, the person who will ultimately be responsible for carrying out the plan should always be part of the team creating this plan and, in many cases, should lead the planning process. Much of the success of an implementation program has to do with the details. Among the most important details is the identification of the areas of the organization and stakeholders that are essential to accomplishing the recommended strategy. Which departments must be involved and who in those departments will participate? How will collaboration across departments be accomplished? Which external stakeholders will be involved and how will they participate in the initiative?

Another important set of details is the establishment of specific milestones and deliverables that each individual manager is responsible for and development of a timeline that defines when those objectives must be met. Detailed plans are then developed for meeting each of the milestones and deliverables. They should add up to (or support) the accomplishment of the overall objectives of the initiative, as described previously.

Ordering Activities

The order of activities associated with most initiatives is important. One tool that is particularly useful for ordering the activities in a detailed action plan is a *Gantt chart*, a type of bar chart developed by Henry Gantt to help with project scheduling.[5] Required activities are entered on a Gantt chart based on what has to happen before they can occur and how long they are expected to take. In addition to assisting in the design of the detailed action plan, the Gantt chart also helps managers understand and focus their energies on activities that might delay the entire project and develop contingency plans in case downstream activities encounter delays. These are often called "bottleneck" activities.

A simplified Gantt chart is shown in Table 7.1 for a hypothetical initiative involving a firm that has decided to sell a new product to existing customers. The firm is in the business of installing plastic shelving designed specifically for the individual needs of large wholesalers. The firm is United States based and has customers in most of the 50 states. It designs the shelving systems for each wholesale location and sends the requirements to a subcontractor in Malaysia, who then manufactures the shelving and ships it back for installation. Customers have no contact with the Malaysian manufacturer. The firm has decided to begin offering plastic bins as a supplement

Table 7.1 Gantt-style chart for new plastic bin initiative

	1	2	3	4	5	6	7	8	9	10	11	12	13	14	15	16	17	18	19	20	21	22	23	24	25
Test phase																									
Assemble initial design team	■	■																							
Discuss requirements with a test customer			■																						
Create preliminary contract with supplier			■																						
Create specifications and place order				■	■																				
Supplier manufactures and ships					■	■																			
Assist customer with bin installation						■	■																		
Evaluate results for firm, customer, supplier							■																		
Full implementation phase																									
Create full staffing plan								■																	
Create resource requirements plan								■																	
Create budget with projected costs/revenues								■	■																
Negotiate permanent contract with supplier									■																
Select marketing person/develop marketing plan									■																
Select/recruit permanent design team									■	■															
Implement marketing plan										■	■														
Acquire full startup requirements including staffing, equipment and supplies, location(s)											■	■													
Engage in business														■	■	■	■	■	■	■	■	■			
Review phase																									
Collect information from supplier, employees, customers																							■	■	
Compile financial information																									■
Conduct review																									■

136

to its shelving systems. This initiative came out of a strategic analysis process in which several past customers expressed frustration when trying to find the right types and sizes of bins to go with the shelving systems after they were installed. Also, during the analysis process, the Malaysian supplier expressed an interest in diversifying into new types of custom-designed plastic products and already has sufficient capacity and expertise to produce the bins. The overall objective for the initiative is that the new storage bins will represent 10 percent of total firm sales in 2 years.

In actual practice, Gantt charts can be very large and require a significant time investment. For example, one particular project in the healthcare industry involved a strategic initiative in which the Gantt charts for each part of the implementation effort, when drafted, filled more than two dozen sheets of 36" × 24" paper. That might seem like a lot of work, but the return on the time invested was enormous. Absent the guidance the Gantt chart provided, the implementation effort would have been highly inefficient and disorganized. Managers sometimes lament that affecting change "is like herding cats." This often does seem to be the case, but it is probably more a result of poor planning than individuals actively resisting strategic efforts.

Budgeting, Communications, and Evaluation

The establishment of a budget is also essential to the accomplishment of the initiative. What resources will be needed, when will they be needed, where will they come from, how much will they cost, and how will the costs be covered? In other words, can the firm achieve its objectives by redirecting current cash flow and resources or will entirely new cash flows and other resources be required? Depending on the nature of the initiative, this could include managers, staff, office space, materials, plant, equipment, technology, IT, marketing, R&D, or any number of other resources. Good budgets always include an estimated time frame for when cash and other resources will be needed. If a Gantt chart is utilized for planning, each of the activities in the Gantt chart is allocated an expected budget and all nonfinancial resources, such as personnel, equipment, and facilities, are identified. If the initiative is revenue generating, these revenues should also be estimated along with their timing. It is very difficult to estimate costs and revenues with accuracy for new initiatives.

Consequently, budgets are reviewed periodically and revised as the initiative is implemented.

Another important consideration during implementation is how to communicate progress to all affected stakeholders. While communication among the implementation team is clearly vital, even projects with good internal communication can suffer if the team fails to connect with affected stakeholders. Communication can take the form of frequent status updates, letting people know how far along the project has come. However, the most effective communications have an education component. As milestones are achieved, firms should ensure that stakeholders are again reminded of why this particular milestone is important and what it will mean once the project is fully implemented. If handled well, this communication process will reinforce feelings of procedural fairness, especially as firm members and other affected stakeholders understand that they were considered during the decision-making process. Such communications are also a form of interactional fairness, as people feel as though they are trusted and treated with respect. Both of these principles will enhance cooperation and thus help with the implementation effort.

As the implementation plan unfolds, there should be times appointed to evaluate progress. When there are problems, evaluation of cause and effect is essential. If activities are behind schedule, it could be that the schedule was unrealistic, that particular activities were not given adequate resources, that these activities or the whole initiative is being poorly managed, or that unforeseen circumstances have caused delays. Similarly, if activities are costing more than anticipated, it could be that estimates were too conservative, that resources are being wasted, that one or more of them is being poorly managed, or that unforeseen circumstances have resulted in unanticipated expenses. Many other reasons exist that could be causing difficulties with timing or costs. The point is that an analysis of cause and effect can help uncover the underlying causes so that managers can devote more attention to resolving them. Also, adjustments to the overall implementation plan may be needed.

Functional-Level Strategies

One of the major challenges of strategy implementation, and strategic management in general, is keeping everything coordinated across all of the functions. A *functional-level strategy* is the strategic approach a firm uses within each of its functional areas (i.e., marketing, operations). Consistent with a systems perspective, each functional area is a piece of the larger system, and coordination among the pieces is essential to successful strategy execution.[6] Table 7.2 provides examples of the various aspects of

Table 7.2 Functional-Level Strategic Priorities in Four Areas

Marketing strategy

- Target customers: broad versus focused, what groups, what regions
- Product positioning: premium, commodity, multiuse, specialty
- Product line mix: mix of complementary products
- Product line breadth: full line or partial line of products
- Pricing: discount, moderate, premium
- Promotion: direct sales, Internet, or through intermediaries, advertising strategy
- Distribution channels: direct to customer, few or many distributors, methods
- Customer service policies: flexibility, nature of response, quality of response
- Market research: sources of information, frequency, uses of market information in other functions

Operations strategy

- Capacity planning: lead demand to ensure availability or lag demand to achieve capacity utilization
- Facility location: proximity to suppliers, customers, labor, technology, natural resources, transportation, and competitors
- Facility layout: continuous or intermittent flow
- Technology and equipment: automation, use of IT, state-of-the-art or standard
- Sourcing arrangements: close relationships with a few versus competitive bid
- Planning and scheduling: made for stock, made to order, flexibility to customer requests
- Quality assurance: acceptance sampling, process control, standards
- Workforce policies: training levels, cross-training

Human resources strategy

- Recruitment: entry-level versus experienced recruits
- Selection: selection criteria and methods
- Performance appraisal: methods, frequency
- Salary and wages: compensation scheme, comparison with competitors
- Benefits: bonuses, employee ownership programs, health, retirement, other benefits
- Personnel actions: new employees, disciplinary, outplacement, early retirements
- Training: type of training, in-house or subcontracted, which employee areas

Information technology strategy

- Hardware capability, integration across firm
- Software capability, integration across firm
- In-house development or subcontractors and consultants
- Use of Internet and Cloud
- Connections with customers and suppliers
- Collection and strategic use of internal, stakeholder, and environmental information
- Rapid or slow adoption of new information technologies

a firm's functional-level strategies for four functional areas found within most firms. The lists are not intended to be exhaustive, and other functional areas will likely be included in the analysis (i.e., R&D, finance).

Well-developed functional-level strategies should be consistent with each other. Is the marketing strategy consistent with the operations strategy? Is the human resources strategy resulting in employees with the right skills, experience, and training to support all of the other functional areas? Does the information technology strategy facilitate communication and coordination across the functional areas and with stakeholders, and is the information provided relevant and timely? Does the R&D strategy result in innovative technologies, products, and services that are consistent with the marketing and operations strategies? Does the financial strategy provide adequate financial resources so that the other functions can succeed with their strategies?

Unfortunately, it is common to find differences of opinion across functional areas regarding the priorities of the firm and the actions it should take. For example, marketing and operations managers frequently advocate very different approaches to the many interdependent decisions that exist between their functional areas. Left to their own devices, with no guidance from executive leadership, it is likely that marketing, over time, will make decisions consistent with a differentiation strategy. Meanwhile, operations managers are likely to seek a low-cost strategy over time as they respond to pressure to improve productivity and reduce costs. These tendencies are completely logical in the absence of leadership regarding priority of trade-offs.

The functional areas should also be consistent with the firm's business model and the strategic initiatives in which it has a part.[7] The business model provides a lot of direction on which types of functional-level strategies a firm should pursue. Similarly, strategic initiatives often require support from many or all of the functional areas and sometimes require adjustments to particular functional-level strategies. In addition to consistency across functional areas, how they are organized within the firm is also important. Organizational structure will be discussed in the next section.

Organizational Structure

A firm's value creation system, and especially its value chain, is tied together by an organization's structure, a system that defines who reports to whom and how work is divided. The formal organizational structure specifies the number and types of departments or groups and provides the formal reporting relationships and lines of communication among internal stakeholders. An organization's structure should be designed to support the business model and strategies of the firm.[8] The underlying assumption is that a strategy–structure fit will lead to superior organization performance.[9] When making decisions about how to structure an organization, it is important to remember the following:

1. Structure is not an end, but a means to an end. The "end" is successful and efficient and effective value creation system.

2. There is no one best structure. A new strategic initiative or a change to the firm's business model may require a corresponding change in structure to avoid administrative inefficiencies; however, the organization's size, strategies, external environment, stakeholder relationships, and management style all influence the appropriateness of a given structure. All structures embody trade-offs.

3. Once in place, the new structure becomes a characteristic of the organization that will serve as a constraint on future strategic choices.

4. Administrative inefficiencies, poor service to customers, communication problems, or employee frustrations may indicate a strategy–structure mismatch.[10]

Standard Structural Forms

Because structures are designed to fit the specific strategies, tasks, and human resources of the firm, practically every organization structure is unique. The simple structures illustrated in this section are important not because an organization will make use of one precisely as it is illustrated, but because they provide visual examples of some of the underlying principles upon which organizational structures are created. One of these principles determines whether people are grouped on the basis of the inputs they provide or the outputs they create. For instance, a *functional structure* (Figure 7.2a) is organized around the functional areas of the firm that are required to manufacture products and create services, such as operations, engineering, marketing, human resources, accounting/finance, and R&D. This sort of structure causes people to become

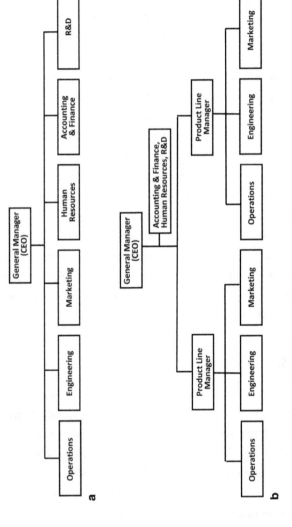

Figure 7.2 Functional and divisional organizational structure

very focused on a particular function in the firm. They become experts, which can enhance the quality and efficiency of what they do.

In contrast, a *divisional structure* (also called a multidivisional structure) is organized around the outputs of the organization. The example found in Figure 7.2b might also be referred to as a product structure because it is organized around the product lines of the firm. For instance, an electronics firm might be divided into handheld electronics, military guidance systems, and home alarm systems. Divisions might also represent customer groups, such as Internet, wholesale, and retail store customers. In addition, they are frequently divided into geographic markets, such as the southern division, northern division, midwestern division, and western division. At an international level, divisions like North America, Pacific Rim, Western Europe, Eastern Europe, and China might make sense. People tend to relate closely to their divisions, which allows them to focus more on creating products and service that satisfy the specific needs of the consumers within their divisions. A disadvantage is that some of the same functions are performed by more than one person or group in a divisional structure. For instance, there is potential for overlap of functions in areas like marketing and engineering. As illustrated in the figure, typically firms try to overcome some of the redundancies by centralizing various functions that can serve multiple divisions, such as accounting, finance, human resources, or R&D.[11]

Structures should be designed, in part, based on where critical decisions should be made—the degree of centralization. In the functional structure example found in Figure 7.2a, the general manager will tend to make all of the key strategic decisions for the firm. In the divisional structure (Figure 7.2b), strategic decisions are shared between the general manager and the divisional managers. The guiding principle is that the divisional manager is best suited to make most of the strategic decisions regarding her/his own division, while the general manager is the best person to make decisions that affect the entire organization.

A *matrix structure* combines elements of both the functional and divisional structures.[12] In the example found in Figure 7.3, functional area managers and divisional product line managers are the organizing elements. Decision-making in a matrix is both decentralized and divided. In the example in the figure, a marketing manager will make decisions

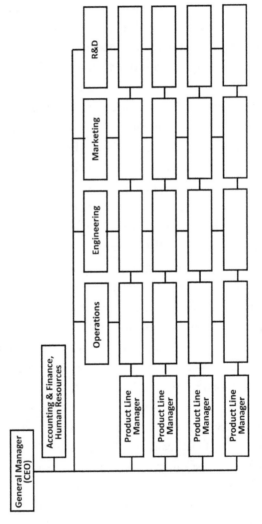

Figure 7.3 Matrix organizational structure

regarding the marketing of products across all of the product lines, but will do so in cooperation with each of the product line managers based on the specific needs in their areas. While this example is based on division into product lines, the left diagonal of a matrix could be based just as easily on type of customer, geographic markets, or even projects in which the firm is engaged. Some observers view the matrix structure as a transition stage between a functional form and a divisional structure, whereas others see the structure as a complex form necessary for complex environments.[13]

Matrix structures are especially common in organizations that experience their workload in the form of projects (i.e., construction firms, consulting firms, architectural firms, movie and television production, and engineering firms). This would put projects on the diagonal instead of product lines. At any given point in time, experts drawn from the functional areas are assigned to various project duties—sometimes spanning across several projects. This provides a lot of flexibility with regard to how human resources are allocated to the productive activities of the firm. The dual-reporting relationships of the matrix structure emphasize the equal importance of functional design performance and service on a particular project to which they are assigned.

Unfortunately, matrix structures can be disconcerting for employees because of the "too many bosses" problem. Not only is it difficult to balance the needs of the different lines of authority and coordinate so many people and schedules, but the sheer number of people who must be involved in decision-making can slow decision processes and add administrative costs. In addition, the overall complexity of the structure can create ambiguity and conflict between managers and employees.

Franchise structures are also very common. A franchise is a contractual agreement between two independent firms that allows one firm to sell the other firm's products or services or operate under an exclusive license that makes use of the franchisor's trademarks in a specific location for a set period of time.[14] Typically the franchisor charges the franchisee a fee for the franchise and also receives a percentage of revenues or profits from each location. Other contract terms vary. McDonalds makes extensive use of a franchise structure. With regard to the three basic structures, it is most like a divisional structure, where each of the franchisees owns and runs what amounts to their own division while having a tight affiliation with the franchising company.

One of the primary advantages of the franchise structure is that the franchisor does not need to obtain as much capital to open a new location because the franchisee typically bears most of the financial burden associated with establishing the business. Consequently, a franchise structure can facilitate a rapid growth strategy. Of course, a franchise structure is also associated with the loss of some of the revenues that might have been obtained at the location of the franchise. In addition, the franchisor loses some control over the franchise, which exposes the franchisor to a certain amount of reputation risk if the franchisee delivers a product or service that is disappointing to customers. Many companies own some of their operating locations while franchising the rest.

More Complex Structures

The increasing need for strategic flexibility in an increasingly competitive domestic and global marketplace has also led to the adoption of alternative, less structured corporate forms of organization. Called by a number of names such as "informal structures," "modular structures," "virtual structures," or "network structures," these are loosely interconnected organizational components with boundaries that are not well defined.[15] Sometimes these types of structures are supplemental to an existing hierarchical structure within the firm (such as those described previously in this chapter). Companies like Microsoft and Reebok have participated with success in such arrangements through alliances and outsourcing.

These sorts of structures involve an extended network of relationships with external stakeholders, including suppliers, subcontractors, distributors, technology partners, and other groups as appropriate. Much or most of the communication and coordination is done electronically. In these types of firms, production can involve many firms simultaneously through a variety of cooperative relationships and joint ventures. They are joined through common goals and allow business components to be recombined into a variety of configurations. However, power structures tend to be nebulous, which can sometimes lead to conflicts, exit of stakeholders from the organization, or opportunistic behavior in which one participant takes advantage of the others.

Foreign Subsidiaries

The manner in which foreign subsidiaries report into the core organizational structure varies from firm to firm. In some multinational organizations, foreign subsidiaries are treated as branch locations, but in others, subsidiaries are much more autonomous.[16] In general, foreign subsidiaries tend to play one of three primary roles:

1. *Local Implementation.* These subsidiaries focus on one country, make minor adjustments to business strategy in order to meet local market needs, execute a strategy planned by corporate management, and have little independence.
2. *Specialized Contribution.* These subsidiaries play a unique role as a member of an interdependent network of subsidiaries, often as a production arm of the network or as a distributor in a particular region.
3. *Global Mandate.* These subsidiaries are responsible for an entire global business. They are more autonomous and have the responsibility for crafting and executing strategies.[17]

The head office is responsible for determining the role each subsidiary will play based on the degree of autonomy required, the need for coordination with other divisions or subsidiaries, and the degree of fit with the overall business model. In addition to their primary responsibilities, foreign subsidiaries are also used for R&D. For example, a subsidiary charged primarily with a local implementation mandate may discover novel solutions to problems or new products that are useful across all of a firm's global businesses.

This chapter has examined tools for implementation planning and strategic control, as well as the organizational structure that ties the value creation system together. The primary focus for all of the first seven chapters of this book has been on strategic planning for value creation systems within business units or divisions. However, sometimes business units are one part of a larger diversified organization, with multiple business units pursuing different business models. The next chapter examines topics particularly relevant at that level of a value creation system.

Notes

1. P. Lorange, M.F.S. Morton, and S. Ghoshal. 1986. *Strategic Control* (St. Paul, MN: West Publishing Company), p. 10.
2. J.S. Harrison and C.H. St. John. 2014. *Foundations in Strategic Management.* 6th ed. (Mason, OH: South-Western), p. 169.
3. P.A. Phillips. 2007. "The Balanced Scorecard and Strategic Control: A Hotel Case Study Analysis," *Service Industries Journal* 27, pp. 731–46; M. Goold and J.J. Quinn. 1990 "The Paradox of Strategic Controls," *Strategic Management Journal* 11, pp. 43–57.
4. Some of this section is adapted from J.S. Harrison and S.M. Thompson. 2015. *Strategic Management of Healthcare Organizations* (New York, NY: Business Expert Press), Chapter 8.
5. W. Clark and H. Gantt. 1922. *The Gantt Chart: A Working Tool of Management* (New York, NY: Ronald Press); J.M. Wilson. 2003. "Gantt Charts: A Contemporary Appreciation," *European Journal of Operational Research* 149, pp. 430–37.
6. D.G. Sirmon, M.A. Hitt, R.D. Ireland, and B.A. Gilbert. 2011. "Resource Orchestration to Create Competitive Advantage: Breadth, Depth, and Life Cycle Effects," *Journal of Management* 37, pp. 1390–412.
7. Y.H. Hsieh and H.M. Chen. 2011. "Strategic Fit among Business Competitive Strategy, Human Resource Strategy, and Reward System," *Academy of Strategic Management Journal* 10, pp. 11–32.
8. J.I. Galan and M.J. Sanchez-Bueno. 2009. "The Continuing Validity of the Strategy-Structure Nexus: New Findings, 1993-2003," *Strategic Management Journal* 30, pp. 1234–43; A.D. Chandler. 1962. *Strategy and Structure: Chapters in the History of the American Industrial Enterprise* (Cambridge, MA: The MIT Press).
9. F.A. Csaszar. 2012. "Organizational Structure as a Determinant of Performance: Evidence from Mutual Funds," *Strategic Management Journal* 33, pp. 611–32.
10. B. Keats and H.M. O'Neill. 2001. "Organizational Structure: Looking through a Strategy Lens." In *The Blackwell Handbook of Strategic Management,* eds. M.A. Hitt, R.E. Freeman, and J.S. Harrison (Oxford, UK: Blackwell Publishers), pp. 520–42; P.R. Lawrence and J.W. Lorsch. 1969. *Organization and Environment* (Homewood, IL: Irwin), pp. 23–39.
11. Keats and O'Neill, "Organizational Structure."
12. G. Kesler and M.H. Schuster. 2009. "Design Your Governance Model to Make the Matrix Work," *People and Strategy* 32, no. 4, pp. 16–25; S.H. Appelbaum, D. Nadeau, and M. Cyr. 2008. "Performance Evaluation in a Matrix Organization: A Case Study," *Industrial and Commercial Training* 40, pp. 295–99.

13. J.R. Galbraith and R.K. Kazanjian. 1986. *Strategy Implementation: Structure, Systems, and Processes* (St. Paul, MN: West Publishing Company).

14. J.G. Combs, D.J. Ketchen, Jr., C.L. Shook, and J.C. Short. 2011. "Antecedents and Consequences of Franchising: Past Accomplishments and Future Challenges," *Journal of Management* 37, no. 1.

15. G. Soda and A. Zaheer. 2012. "A Network Perspective on Organizational Architecture: Performance Effects of the Interplay of Formal and Informal Organization," *Strategic Management Journal* 33, pp. 751–71; M.A. Schilling and H.K. Steensma. 2001. "The Use of Modular Organizational Forms: An Industry-Level Analysis," *Academy of Management Journal* 44, pp. 1149–68.

16. R. Mudambi. 2011. "Hierarchy, Coordination and Innovation in the Multinational Enterprise," *Global Strategy Journal* 1, pp. 317–23; N. Nohria and S. Ghoshal. 1997. *The Differentiated Network* (San Francisco, CA: Jossey-Bass).

17. J.M. Birkinshaw and A.J. Morrison. 1995. "Configurations of Strategy and Structure in Subsidiaries of Multinational Corporations," *Journal of International Business Studies* 26, pp. 729–54.

CHAPTER 8

Strategic Management of the Corporate-Level System

Many large and even some smaller firms have multiple business units pursuing different business models. That is, the business units manufacture different products and provide a variety of services based on different asset uses to various market segments, and they do so with value creation objectives and growth strategies that are not the same as other business units. They are diversified. While much of the material in the previous chapters is applicable in diversified firms, there are special management challenges associated with these complex value creation systems.

The purpose of this chapter is to provide some useful perspectives and tools for managing diversified firms. Basically, it answers the question of how corporate-level actions can enhance (or reduce) the ability of the firm to create value for stakeholders. It discusses the way business units can be related to each other and provides a rationale for building synergies in the firm's value creation system based on similarities among them. It also discusses specific tactics firms use to diversify and how they are structured from a corporate-level perspective.

Corporate-Level Strategies

Corporate-level strategies tend to fall into four basic types: concentration, vertical integration, unrelated diversification, and related diversification. Although not all firms can be classified neatly into one of these types, the categories provide a useful framework for discussing the strengths and weaknesses of each of the strategic approaches.

Concentration

Companies engaged in a single business area are pursuing a type of corporate-level strategy called *concentration*. Federal Express, Domino's Pizza, Lands' End, and Delta Airlines (as of the time of this writing) are examples of firms that are pursuing a concentration strategy. It should be noted that often large organizations may have a relatively small business or two in another area, but as long as 90 percent or more of their revenues are from one business area they can still be treated as concentrators.

The profitability of a concentration strategy is largely dependent on the industry in which a firm is involved. When industry conditions are attractive, the strengths of a concentration strategy are readily apparent. A single business approach allows an organization to master one business area due to specialization, and since all resources are directed at doing one thing well, the organization's value chain is likely to be more efficient and effective. Also, a concentration strategy can prevent the proliferation of management levels and staff functions that are often associated with large multibusiness firms and that add overhead costs. In addition, a concentration strategy allows the firm to invest its profits back into one business, rather than having to spread investments across multiple business units.

On the other hand, concentration strategies entail several risks, especially when environments are unstable. Since the firm is dependent on one business area to sustain itself, change can dramatically reduce the performance of a firm's value creation system. For example, the entry of new competitors, new government regulations, or a negative change in public opinion about a product can alter the effectiveness of a firm's business model. Similarly, managers will find it difficult to increase the amount of value created for stakeholders if the industry is in decline or a product becomes obsolete. Some organizations are never able to duplicate earlier successes, so they enter a stage of decline and are acquired or go bankrupt. The situation is even more difficult because firms that have been pursuing concentration have experience in only the business area, which limits their ability to switch to other areas when times get tough.

Concentration strategies can also lead to uneven cash flows and volatility in profitability. While the business is growing, the firm may find itself in a "cash-poor" situation, since growth often entails additional investments in capital equipment and marketing. On the other hand, once growth levels off, the firm is likely to find itself in a "cash-rich" situation, with limited opportunities for profitable investment in the business itself. In fact, this may be one of the most important reasons that organizations in mature markets begin to diversify.[1] Having exhausted all reasonable opportunities to reinvest cash in innovation, renewal, or revitalization, managers may look to other areas for growth.

Many successful organizations abandon their concentration strategies at some point due to market saturation, increased competition, or some other reason. In these situations, corporate strategy evolves from concentration on a single business to some form of vertical integration or diversification.

Vertical Integration

Vertical integration, introduced in Chapter 3, is the term used to describe the extent to which a firm is involved in multiple stages of an industry supply chain.[2] An industry supply chain is similar to a firm's value chain, but at an industry level. All tangible goods begin with some sort of raw material. For example, steel begins as iron ore, which is extracted from the earth and then goes through a variety of processes until it is ultimately formed into final products that are either consumed as is (i.e., steel needles) or combined into other products (i.e., anything with a steel component in it). Backward vertical integration moves the firm one more step toward the creation or extraction of a raw material and forward vertical integration moves the firm one more step toward the ultimate consumer.

Some industries, such as steel and wood production, contain many firms that are highly vertically integrated. In other industries, such as apparel, vertical integration is limited, and most organizations are only involved in one or two stages. Firms may pursue vertical integration for a variety of reasons, including increased efficiency, increased control over the quality of supplies or the way a product is marketed, better or more complete information about suppliers or markets, greater opportunity for product differentiation through coordinated effort, or simply because they believe they can enhance profits through assuming one of the functions that was previously performed by another company.[3] For example, Walt Disney Company is involved in movie and television studios, movie distribution, broadcast and cable networks, theme parks, and retailing with the intention of controlling their product from concept to customers.

Transaction cost economics, which is the study of economic exchanges and their costs, provides a cost perspective on vertical integration that helps explain when it may be desirable.[4] From a transaction cost perspective, firms can either negotiate on the open market for the products and services they need or create these products and services themselves (e.g., vertically integrate). If an organization can obtain required resources from a competitive open market without allocating an undue amount of time or other resources to the contracting process or contract enforcement, then it is probably prudent to buy from the market instead of vertically integrating. However, sometimes transaction costs associated with contract creation and enforcement are high enough to encourage a firm to pursue vertical integration by producing the product or service in-house. This is called a market failure, meaning that the market is a relatively unattractive alternative.

Several situations can lead to this sort of market failure—four of the most common will be described here. First, if the future is highly uncertain, it may be too costly or impossible to identify all of the situations that may occur and to incorporate all of these possibilities into a contract. Second, if only one or very few firms supply a particular good or service, it is highly probable that those suppliers will negotiate extremely favorable contract terms to the detriment of their buyers. At some point, many firms just decide to either buy one of the suppliers or create the needed product or service in-house. Third, if one party to a transaction has more knowledge about the transaction or a series of transactions than another party, it will tend to use this information to its advantage in negotiating a contract.

Finally, if a supplier must invest in a specific asset in order to produce what is needed to provide a good or service to its customer, and if that asset can only be used for one purpose, the supplier must charge a very high price in order to account for the risk associated with the investment. That is, if the customer decides not to order the product or service anymore, the supplier will be left with an asset that may no longer have much value. This situation is called *asset specificity*. For example, assume that a bicycle manufacturing company needs a special titanium alloy bicycle frame and the frame supplier will have to build new machinery to produce it. In addition, the new machinery would be useful only for work with the new material. The supplier will have to charge a large premium for the frame in order to offset this risk. At some point, the customer simply decides to build the machinery and produce the bicycle frame itself.

Although there are clearly times when vertical integration is an attractive option, such as when transaction costs are very high, it is often a bad idea. This is because vertical integration often requires substantially different skills than those currently possessed by the firm. A firm that can master one stage of the industry supply chain will not necessarily excel in other stages. Consider, for example, a clothing manufacturer that vertically integrates by acquiring a textiles manufacturer. The knowledge, capabilities, and physical resources for producing clothing (e.g., marketing research, clothing design and sewing, typically by hand) are completely different from what is required for producing textiles (large batch manufacturing using sophisticated technology and large-scale economies). In this regard, vertical integration is similar to unrelated diversification, which will be discussed in the next section. In addition, vertical integration can link a firm tightly to adjacent businesses that are unprofitable, increase the costs of coordination, and limit the amount of valuable information a firm gets from its suppliers or customers.[5]

Diversification

Firms pursue diversification for a number of reasons in an effort to create new value for stakeholders.[6] From a strategic perspective, managers may be trying to reduce risk by spreading investments across businesses that are subject to different environmental forces. This could also stabilize cash flows. Sometimes managers are trying to improve growth in sales or income by investing in new businesses that are growing faster or are in more profitable industries. They could also be seeking new applications of their current resources and capabilities, resulting in synergy between the new businesses and existing businesses. Or they could be searching for opportunities to learn new technologies. It is also possible that firms just have a lot of financial slack (i.e., debt capacity or excess cash) and managers feel pressure from shareholders to do something useful with it.

Of course, managers are human, and sometimes they pursue diversification for their own personal enrichment. For example, a CEO could institute a diversification plan for the firm in an effort to grow their own power and status, or to give the board a reason to increase her/his compensation, or because of a craving for a more interesting and challenging management environment. Motivations of this type can also align with strategic reasons such as those mentioned previously; however, when they do not, an agency problem exists.

Diversification can be divided into two broad categories. Related diversification implies organizational involvement in activities that are somehow related to the dominant or core business of the organization, often through common markets or similar technologies. Unrelated diversification does not depend on any particular pattern of relatedness.

Unrelated Diversification

Unrelated diversification was once a very popular strategy, especially in the United States. Firms like General Electric built huge portfolios of disparate businesses, and financial investors applauded their efforts. However, over time the financial performance of these types of firms was not as high as expected, and many of them began to divest businesses that were not closely related to their core businesses.

Divestitures have been found to improve firm performance, especially when they are part of a well-planned restructuring.[7] One type of divestiture is a *sell-off*, in which a business unit is sold to another firm or group of investors. *Spin-offs* are another form of divestiture. One form of spin-off gives current shareholders a proportional number of shares in the spun-off business. The key advantage of a spin-off relative to other divestiture options is that shareholders still have the option of retaining ownership in the spun-off business. Initial public offerings (IPOs) can also be used to spin off a business. For example, eBay determined that its Skype Internet-phone business was not a good fit with its core operations. The company could not find an offer attractive enough to sell off the business, so it initiated an IPO.[8] However, Skype didn't remain independent for long. Microsoft soon acquired the spun-off company.

Large, unrelated diversified firms still exist. Tata Group, based in India, is an Indian conglomerate with operations in more than 80 countries across Europe, Asia, Australia, North America, and South America. Tata operates in many business sectors, including communications and information technology, engineering, materials, services, energy, consumer products, and chemicals. Royal Philips of the Netherlands has also diversified into a wide variety of largely unrelated industries, including health care, lighting, health and wellness, appliances, coffee, personal care products, and electronics.

In theory, unrelated diversified firms should be able to achieve high returns through financial economies. One type of economy comes from the ability of the firm to allocate capital to those business areas in the organization that have the highest potential for growth and profitability. Another type of financial economy occurs as a firm purchases another organization and restructures the acquired company's assets. A final type of financial economy comes from the large size of the conglomerate firm, which in theory should lead to more attractive financing alternatives (i.e., a lower interest rate on debt).

In spite of the strength of the logic behind financial economies, much of the research on firms in the United States has demonstrated that unrelated diversification reduces financial performance.[9] In fact, there is less unrelated diversification now than there was several decades ago. Unrelated diversification places significant demands on corporate-level executives due to increased complexity and technological changes across industries. In fact, it is very difficult for a manager to understand each of the core technologies and appreciate the special requirements of each of the individual units in an unrelated diversified firm. Consequently, the effectiveness of management may be reduced.

Although unrelated diversification may be a poorly performing strategy overall, some firms perform well. Royal Philips and Hitachi of Japan have enjoyed success with the strategy. In addition, some researchers have found that high levels of diversification may lead to higher financial performance in less developed countries.[10] Large firms like Tata Group seem able to allocate resources to profitable business areas more effectively than the inefficient capital markets that often exist in their own countries. Also, unrelated diversified firms, due to their vast resources, may be able to overcome some of the problems associated with a poorly developed infrastructure. For instance, a large, highly diversified firm may have skills and resources in business areas such as transportation, construction, or power generation that can help its businesses overcome problems in these areas.

Related Diversification and Synergy

Some form of relatedness among diversified businesses, as opposed to no relatedness at all, can lead to the creation of additional value for stakeholders.[11] *Related diversification* is based on similarities that exist among the products, services, markets, or resource conversion processes of two businesses. Honda Motor Company pursues a related diversification strategy. Honda's diversification strategy focuses on developing and manufacturing products that make use of its highly efficient internal combustion engines. The company offers a wide variety of automobiles in various styles suited to the countries in which they are sold. Honda's motorcycle business includes all-terrain vehicles and personal watercraft. In addition to its automobile and motorcycle businesses, Honda produces a line of power products such as snowblowers, tillers, lawn mowers, and outboard boat engines.

Relatedness comes in two forms: tangible and intangible.[12] *Tangible relatedness* means that the organization has the opportunity to use the same physical resources for multiple purposes. Tangible relatedness can lead to synergy through resource sharing. For example, if two similar products are manufactured in the same plant, they can benefit from operating synergy. Other examples of synergy resulting from tangible relatedness include (1) using the same marketing or distribution channels for multiple related products, (2) buying similar raw materials for related products through a centralized purchasing office to gain purchasing economies, (3) providing corporate training programs to employees from different divisions who are all engaged in the same type of work, (4) advertising multiple products simultaneously, and (5) manufacturing in the same plants.

Intangible relatedness occurs any time capabilities developed in one part of a firm's value creation system can be applied to another area. For example, Campbell Soup has applied its skills in manufacturing and packaging soup to a variety of other products. Synergy based on intangible resources such as brand name or management skills and knowledge may be more conducive to the creation of a sustainable competitive advantage, since intangible resources are hard to imitate and are never used up.

If conditions are right, relatedness among products and services can lead to *synergy*, which means that the whole is greater than the sum of its parts.[13] In other words, one organization should be able to produce two related products or services more efficiently than two organizations each producing one of the products or services on its own. But even if relatedness exists, synergy *has to be created*, which means that the two related businesses must fit together *and* that organizational managers must work at creating efficiencies from the combination process. Furthermore, the benefits from synergy have to exceed the costs of creating it. Otherwise, increasing coordination costs have the potential to offset potential synergistic gains from related diversification.[14]

Two types of fit facilitate the creation of synergy: strategic fit and organizational fit. *Strategic fit* refers to the effective matching of strategic organizational capabilities. For example, if two organizations in two related businesses combine their resources, but they are both strong in the same areas and weak in the same areas, then the potential for synergy is diminished. Once combined, they will continue to exhibit the same capabilities. However, if one of the organizations is strong in R&D but lacks marketing power, while the other organization is weak in R&D but strong in marketing, then there is real potential for both organizations to be better off—if managed properly. *Organizational fit* occurs when two organizations or business units have similar management processes, cultures, systems, and structures.[15] Organizational fit makes businesses compatible, which facilitates resource sharing, communication, and transference of knowledge and skills across the firm's value chain. Strategic fit and organizational fit dramatically increase the likelihood that synergy will be created between two related businesses.

Assuming that firm leaders have decided to pursue diversification as a corporate strategy, they must still decide on the method that will be followed to carry it out. Methods for pursuing diversification will be discussed in the next section.

Tactics for Pursuing Diversification

Once an organization has decided to pursue a diversification strategy, it can follow one of three basic approaches to carry it out: an internal venture to develop the new business on its own, an acquisition, or a strategic alliance such as a joint venture.

Internal Ventures

An internal venture is a diversification method that relies largely on internal resources and capabilities. Since only the core organization is involved, management has greater control over the progress of the venture. Furthermore, proprietary information need not be shared with other companies that might otherwise be involved in the venture, and all profits are retained within the firm. However, the risks of failure are high and even successful ventures take many years to become profitable. In fact, the slow speed of internal ventures often causes managers to think seriously about acquisitions when they want to diversify their firms.[16] If a firm acquires an existing business, it gains immediate entrance into the new business area. Nevertheless, acquisitions come with their own risks and problems, as the next section will demonstrate.

Mergers and Acquisitions

As an alternative to internal ventures, some firms choose to buy diversification in the form of acquisitions. In fact, they are often considered a substitute for internal innovation.[17] Mergers occur any time two organizations combine into one. For example, Lockheed and Martin Marietta merged to create a new company called Lockheed Martin. Acquisitions, in which one organization buys a controlling interest in the stock of another organization or buys it outright from its owners, are the most common type of mergers.

Acquisitions are a relatively quick way to satisfy needs in the firm's value creation system that were identified through analysis and assessment. For example, they may be used to enter new markets, acquire new products or services, learn new technologies, acquire needed skills, vertically integrate, broaden markets geographically, or increase market share in existing businesses. Unfortunately, acquisitions tend to reduce financial performance, especially in the short term.[18] This may be because the acquiring firm pays too much for its target, or because interest expenses increase due to the borrowing that is almost always associated with an acquisition. Low performance could also be due to high advisory fees and other transaction costs, high turnover following the acquisition, depressed innovation levels, a lack of strategic or organizational fit between the acquiring and acquired firms, or simply because the managers engaged in the acquisition process are so distracted with it that they lose track of other businesses within the firm.

This does not mean that all mergers are doomed to failure. Fortunately, researchers have been able to identify factors that seem to be associated with successful mergers. They involve only low-to-moderate amounts of debt, a high level of relatedness between the two companies, friendly negotiations (no resistance), strategic and organizational fit, careful selection of and negotiations with the acquired firm (due diligence), use of cash as opposed to stock to make the acquisition, and a strong financial position going into the deal.[19] It may also take time for the benefits of an acquisition to become evident. For example, it may take a major restructuring of the firm to allow all of the potential synergies among businesses to be unlocked.[20]

Many of the diversification objectives sought by organizations through acquisitions are also available through joint ventures and alliances, which is the topic of the next section.

Joint Ventures and Alliances

Previously strategic alliances were described as any time two or more organizations join for a common purpose. Alliances may be formed to develop new products or services, enter new markets, influence government bodies, conduct research, improve technology, or for a host of other reasons. Strategic alliances of all types are very popular. When firms come together to form a legally independent company, then the alliance is typically called a joint venture. For the purposes of this section, the word *alliances* refers to both joint ventures that involve equity and other types of alliances.

Alliances can help organizations achieve many of the same diversification objectives that are sought through mergers and acquisitions. They can lead to improved sales growth and increased earnings or provide balance to a portfolio of businesses. However, one of the strongest rationales for forming an alliance is resource sharing. Since alliances involve more than one company, they can draw on a much larger resource and capability base and can thus address some of the weak areas found in a firm's value creation system. The resources that are most likely to be transferable across companies are:

1. *Marketing.* Companies can gain marketing information and resources not easily identified by outsiders, such as knowledge of competition, customer behavior, specific industry conditions, and distribution channels.
2. *Technology.* Those participating in an alliance can learn from partners or develop technological skills and specific knowledge that is not generally available.
3. *Raw Materials and Components.* Some alliances may be formed to provide partner companies access to rare or difficult-to-obtain resources needed in the value chain.
4. *Financial.* Combined firm strength may allow the partnering firms to obtain external capital under favorable terms.
5. *Managerial.* Alliance participants can use specific managerial and entrepreneurial capabilities and skills, usually in conjunction with other resources.
6. *Political.* Sometimes alliances are important to entering developing countries (i.e., China, India) because of either formal or informal political requirements; others are formed to gain preferential treatment from regulators or government leaders.

Because of the advantages associated with resource sharing, alliances can enhance speed of entry into a new field or market because of the expanded base of resources from which ventures can draw. Alliances also spread the risk of failure among all of the participants. That is, a failure will result in a smaller loss to each alliance partner than it would to an organization that pursues the venture on its own. Alliances can also increase strategic flexibility by allowing a firm to more easily leave a business and invest resources elsewhere.[21] This is especially true for alliances that do not involve equity. Consequently, compared to mergers or internal venturing, alliances are sometimes considered a less risky diversification option.

In spite of their strategic strengths, alliances are limiting, in that each organization only has partial control over the partnership and enjoys only part of the benefits. Alliances can also create high administrative costs associated with developing the agreement and managing the venture once it is undertaken. As in mergers and acquisitions, lack of organizational fit between partners has the potential to reduce cooperation and lead to alliance failure. Also, if one party to a multifirm alliance decides to withdraw, the success of the alliance may be put in jeopardy.

Alliances also entail a risk of opportunism by participating firms. For instance, a company may gain knowledge or contacts from its alliance partner, which it can then use in future competition with that same partner after severing the relationship. Good written contracts can help to alleviate but cannot eliminate this risk. Alliances with firms in other countries add even more risks due to potential problems such as miscommunication (especially where languages are different), differences in management systems and styles between the firms, or lack of understanding of the political, economic, and legal environments of the partner firms.

Successful alliances require careful planning and execution. During the stage in which an alliance is formed, three attributes are vital to selecting a good partner. The first is partner complementarity, which means that each partner contributes nonoverlapping resources to the partnership.[22] Second, firms should be compatible in terms of their cultures and work arrangements. Third, each of the parties to the alliance should demonstrate a commitment to it. These three features increase the probability that an alliance will lead to the creation of more value than any of the parties could create independently. In addition, postformation success depends on the effective use of coordinating mechanisms that allow the companies to take maximum advantage of the resources that are available to them. In addition, the development of trust and effective conflict resolution mechanisms is essential to success.[23]

For all of the corporate-level strategies and diversification tactics, skill in execution is of critical importance to increasing the amount of value created for stakeholders. Even strategies that might be considered less attractive can be successful if they are executed well.

Organization Structure at the Corporate Level

Most diversified firms use some form of the divisional structure described in Chapter 7. For firms that use acquisitions as a primary growth strategy, the firms they acquire often continue to operate as separate divisions within the firm's structure, with very little integration of activities, at least for the first few years. When a firm is broadly diversified, with several businesses in its portfolio, management may choose to form strategic business units (SBUs), with each unit incorporating businesses that have something in common. Commonality can result from a number of factors, including similarities in technology, products, customers, raw materials, or locations. The related businesses are grouped into SBUs in order to facilitate information sharing and coordination of related activities. Managers of the related businesses report to an SBU manager, who reports to corporate headquarters. Figure 8.1 contains an example of a small SBU structure with only two SBUs and three divisions per SBU. In this example only the industrial engines division shows the functional areas below the division level—the other divisions are assumed to be similarly structured.

Many large diversified firms have several SBUs and divisions. Unlike the illustration in the figure, each of the divisions could be structured differently. For example, instead of being functionally structured (as shown), a division could have its own divisional structure organized around product groups, customer types, or geographic regions. A division within the division could also be structured in a matrix form. Structures within divisions are created so as to best implement that division's business model. It is possible, then, for one large diversified firm to have every basic type of structure represented in its organization chart.

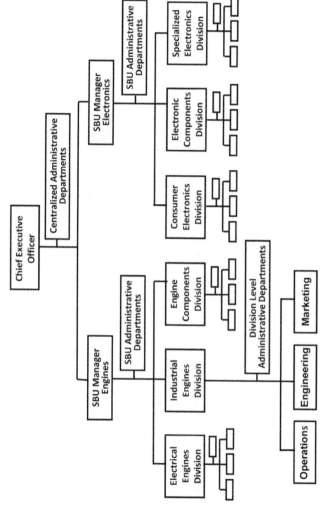

Figure 8.1 Strategic business unit (SBU) structure

Although the SBU structure in the figure is small, it is still helpful for explaining some of the important aspects of the structure with regard to creating synergy across the firm's entire value creation system. As mentioned previously in this chapter, the creation of synergy requires some form of relatedness across business units as well as actions from managers to realize it. A firm that operates its divisions with complete independence from one another may enjoy some aspects of financial synergy because of size, debt capacity, and so forth. However, other types of synergy will not occur. In the example in Figure 8.1, three divisions are found in the engines SBU, and all of them engage in businesses related to some aspect of engines.

To gain synergies from this particular structural form, the SBU manager should initiate and oversee programs to increase communications among the related divisions, such as linked IT systems. Innovations, patents, value chain information, data regarding the external environment, and other pertinent knowledge should be shared. If some of the same raw materials and other supplies are used in more than one division, the purchasing processes can be combined. The components division may also supply the other two divisions. If this is the case, design teams can be created with people from both divisions for new engines or new components. Transfers of employees and managers across divisions can also help with information transfer and capability development, as well as providing more opportunities for advancement. The point is that synergy has to be created through deliberate action.

The Ongoing Strategic Management Process

The strategic management process is never complete. Collection of strategic intelligence is ongoing, as is management and assessment of that information. Periodically managers take time out from their normal work routines to engage in a more intensive strategic planning process; however, a well-developed strategic control process ensures that the initiatives associated with the strategic plan remain in the forefront of the minds of managers.

This book began by laying a theoretical foundation for strategic management based on economics, the resource-based perspective, and stakeholder theory, with systems theory playing an integrative role. Next came a discussion of the strategic direction of the firm upon which all of a firm's strategies and implementation plans are built. Analysis of the internal resources of a firm and its value chain came next, followed by analysis of the external environment. The next topic was assessment of all of the information that was gathered so that strategic initiatives could be developed. Then came the tools for carrying out the initiatives: implementation planning built inside a system of strategic controls. Organizational structures then provided a layer of understanding regarding how a firm's value creation systems are held together through reporting relationships and the division of work. Finally, this chapter went one level higher in the organization and discussed both strategies and structures for managing diversified businesses—systems made up of business units that were described in earlier chapters. In each case theories and methods were built upon the foundations laid in previous chapters.

The most evident guiding philosophy of this book is that organizations exist to provide value to their stakeholders. As the Business Roundtable statement presented in Chapter 1 demonstrated, many of the world's most influential CEOs agree with this philosophy. Envisioning the firm as a value creation system is an effective way to organize the strategic management process so that more stakeholder value can be created.

Notes

1. R. Guo. 2011. "What Drives Firms to Be More Diversified," *Journal of Finance and Accountancy* 6, pp. 1–10; H.I. Ansoff. 1965. *Corporate Strategy: An Analytical Approach to Business Policy for Growth and Expansion* (New York, NY: McGraw-Hill), pp. 129–30.
2. A. Chongvilaivan and J. Hur. 2012. "Trade Openness and Vertical Integration: Evidence from the U.S. Manufacturing Sector," *Southern Economic Journal* 78, pp. 1242–64.
3. L.F. Mesquita, J. Anand, and T.H. Brush. 2008. "Comparing the Resource-Based and Relational Views: Knowledge Transfer and Spillover in Vertical Alliances," *Strategic Management Journal* 29, pp. 913–41; K.R. Harrigan. 1984. "Formulating Vertical Integration Strategies," *Academy of Management Review* 9, p. 639.
4. S.H. Seggie. 2012. "Transaction Cost Economics in International Marketing: A Review and Suggestions for the Future," *Journal of International*

Marketing 20, no. 2, pp. 49–71; O.E. Williamson. 1975. *Markets and Hierarchies: Analysis and Antitrust Implications* (New York, NY: The Free Press); O.E. Williamson. 1985. *The Economic Institutions of Capitalism* (New York, NY: The Free Press).

5. Harrigan, "Formulating Vertical Integration Strategies."

6. W.P. Wan, R.E. Hoskisson, J.C. Short, and D.W. Yiu. 2011. "Resource-Based Theory and Corporate Diversification: Accomplishments and Opportunities," *Journal of Management* 37, pp. 1335–68; Guo, "What Drives Firms to Be More Diversified?"

7. D. Lee and R. Madhavan. 2010. "Divestiture and Firm Performance: A Meta-analysis," *Journal of Management* 36, pp. 1345–71; C. Markides. 1992. "Consequences of Corporate Refocusing: Ex Ante Evidence," *Academy of Management Journal* 35, pp. 398–412.

8. G.A. Fowler. 2009. "EBay to Unload Skype in IPO, Citing Poor Fit," *Wall Street Journal*, April 15, B1.

9. M. Schommer, A. Richter, and A. Karna. 2019. "Does the Diversification-Firm Performance Relationship Change Over Time? A Meta-Analytic Review," *Journal of Management Studies* 56, pp. 270–98; L.E. Palich, L.B. Cardinal, and C.C. Miller. 2000. "Curvilinearity in the Diversification⬛performance Linkage: An Examination of Over Three Decades," *Strategic Management Journal* 21, pp. 155–74.

10. C.-J. Chen and C.-M.J. Yu. 2012. "Managerial Ownership, Diversification and Firm Performance," *International Business Review* 21, pp. 518–34; W.P. Wan and R.E. Hoskisson. 2003. "Home Country Environments, Corporate Diversification Strategies, and Firm Performance," *Academy of Management Journal* 46, pp. 27–45; R.E. Hoskisson, R.A. Johnson, D. Yiu, and W.P. Wan. 2001. "Restructuring Strategies of Diversified Business Groups: Difference Associated with Country Institutional Environments." In: *The Blackwell Handbook of Strategic Management*, M.A. Hitt, R.E. Freeman, and J.S. Harrison, eds. (Oxford, UK: Blackwell Publishers), p. 444.

11. Schommer, et al., "Does the Diversification-Firm Performance Relationship Change Over Time?"

12. T. Ravichandran, Y. Liu, S. Han, and I. Hasan. 2009. "Diversification and Firm Performance: Exploring the Moderating Effects of Information Technology Spending," *Journal of Management* 25, pp. 205–40; M.E. Porter. 1985. *Competitive Advantage: Creating and Sustaining Superior Performance* (New York, NY: The Free Press).

13. B. Melnikas. 2011. "Knowledge Economy: Synergy Effects, Interinstitutional Interaction and Internationalization Processes," *Engineering Economics* 22, pp. 367–79; G. Hoberg and G. Phillips. 2010. "Product Market

Synergies and Competition in Mergers and Acquisitions: A Text-Based Analysis," *Review of Financial Studies* 23, pp. 3773–811.

14. Y.M. Zhou. 2011. "Synergy, Coordination Costs, and Diversification Choices," *Strategic Management Journal* 32, pp. 624–39.

15. M.A. Hitt, J.S. Harrison, and R.D. Ireland. 2001. *Mergers and Acquisitions: A Guide to Creating Value for Stakeholders* (Oxford, UK: Oxford University Press); D.B. Jemison and S.B. Sitkin. 1986. "Corporate Acquisitions: A Process Perspective," *Academy of Management Review* 11, pp. 145–63.

16. K. Ruckman. 2008. "Externally Sourcing Research through Acquisition: Should It Supplement or Substitute for Internal Research?" *Industry and Innovation* 15, pp. 627–45.

17. M.A. Hitt, R.E. Hoskisson, R.D. Ireland, and J.S. Harrison. 1991. "Effects of Acquisitions on R&D Inputs and Outputs," *Academy of Management Journal* 34, pp. 693–706.

18. E. King and L. Irayanti. 2019. "How Mergers and Acquisitions Affect Firm Performance and Its Quality," *Journal of Accounting, Finance & Auditing Studies* 5, pp. 42–53; D.K. Oler, J.S. Harrison, and M.R. Allen. 2008. "The Danger of Misinterpreting Short-Window Event Study Findings in Strategic Management Research: An Empirical Investigation Using Horizontal Acquisitions," *Strategic Organization* 6, no. 2, pp. 151–84.

19. Hitt, Harrison, and Ireland, *Mergers and Acquisitions*; J. Haleblian, C.E. Devers, G. McNamara, M.A. Carpenter, and R.B. Davison. 2009. "Taking Stock of What We Know About Mergers and Acquisitions: A Review and Research Agenda," *Journal of Management* 35, pp. 469–502; Hitt, Harrison, and Ireland, *Mergers and Acquisitions*.

20. H.G. Barkema and M. Schijven. 2008. "Toward Unlocking the Full Potential of Acquisitions: The Role of Organizational Restructuring," *Academy of Management Journal* 51, pp. 696–722.

21. B.R. Barringer and J.S. Harrison. 2000. "Walking a Tightrope: Creating Value through Interorganizational Relationships," *Journal of Management* 26, pp. 367–403

22. J. Bundy, R.M. Vogel, and M.A. Zachary. 2018. "Organization-Stakeholder Fit: A Dynamic Theory of Cooperation, Compromise, and Conflict between and Organization and Its Stakeholders," *Strategic Management Journal* 39, pp. 476–501.

23. P. Kale and H. Singh. 2009. "Managing Strategic Alliances: What Do We Know Now, and Where Do We Go from Here?" *Academy of Management Perspectives* 23, no. 3, pp. 45–62; P.W. Beamish and N.C. Lupton. 2009. "Managing Joint Ventures," *Academy of Management Perspectives* 32, no. 2, pp. 75–94.

About the Author

Jeffrey S. Harrison is a University Distinguished Educator and the W. David Robbins Chair of Strategic Management at the Robins School of Business, University of Richmond. Prior to his current appointment he was the Fred G. Peelen Professor of Global Hospitality Strategy at Cornell University. Dr Harrison's research interests include strategic management and stakeholder theory. Much of his research has been published in top academic journals such as the *Academy of Management Journal, Academy of Management Review, Strategic Management Journal, Journal of Management, Business Ethics Quarterly,* and *Journal of Business Ethics.* His work has been cited over 20,000 times, according to Google Scholar. This is his 13th book. Dr Harrison serves as a section editor for the *Journal of Business Ethics* and on several editorial boards, including that of the *Strategic Management Journal, Business Ethics Quarterly,* and *Academy of Management Review.* He has served as an editor for special issues on stakeholder themes at several journals, including the *Academy of Management Journal, Academy of Management Review, Business & Society,* and *Academy of Management Executive.* He also served as chair of the Stakeholder Strategy Interest Group—a group he helped organize—at the Strategic Management Society.

Dr Harrison has provided consulting and executive training services to dozens of organizations in the United States, South America, and Asia on a wide range of strategic, entrepreneurial, and other business issues. His client list has included Lockheed Martin, Siemens Westinghouse, American Express, Southdown, Bell Technologies, and Volvo Group North America.

Index

Firm (*continued*)
  knowledge and learning activities, 78
  performance measures, 2–3
  value chain, 74
  value creation system, 1, 60
Force field analysis, 116
Foreign subsidiaries, 147
Fortune publishes, 68
Franchise structures, 145
Functional-level strategy, 138–140
Functional organizational structure, 142

Game, rules of, 123–124
Gantt-style chart, 135, 136
Global product/market strategy, 52
Glocalization, 52
Gross domestic product (GDP), 98

Heterogeneity, 70
Human resources, 80
Hybrid transnational, 52

Implementation planning, 134–140
Independent boards, 71
Industrial organization economics, 13–15
Influencers stakeholders, 96
Information technology (IT), 78
Initial public offerings (IPOs), 156–157
Intangible relatedness, 159
Intangible resources, 64
Interactional justice, 20
Interlocking directors, 70
Internal capabilities, 109–112
Internal growth strategies, 53
Internal operations management, 75
Internal resource, 83–85, 109–112
  analysis, 72
  employees, 68–69
  financial resources, 65–67
  managers and governance structure, 69–73
  sustainable competitive advantage, 62–64

Internal stakeholders, 40
Internal venture, 160
International growth strategy, 55
International product/market strategy, 51–55

Joint alliances, 161–164
Joint ventures, 121, 161–164

Knowledge and learning, 77, 78

Legal support, 80
Logistics, 73
Low-cost leadership strategy, 47–49
Lumpy, 24

Managers/governance structure, 69–73
Market
  definition of, 45
  development strategy, 53
  penetration, 53
  management, 76
Matrix organizational structure, 143, 144
McKinsey survey, 16
Mergers/acquisitions, 160–161
Mission and vision, 40–41
Multidomestic product/market strategy, 55

Natural Resources Defense Council, 124
Network centrality, 81
Nongovernmental organization (NGO), 81, 89, 96, 97, 122–123
Nonmarket strategies, 122–124

Organization structure, 164–166
Organizational justice, 18, 31
Organizational learning, 78
Organizational resource interconnectedness, 26
Organizational slack, 113
Organizational structure, 140–147
Ownership, 134

OTHER TITLES IN THE STRATEGIC MANAGEMENT COLLECTION

John A. Pearce II, Villanova University, *Editor*

- *Strategic Management: An Executive Perspective* by Cornelius A. de Kluyver
- *Strategic Management of Healthcare Organizations: A Stakeholder Management Approach* by Jeffrey S. Harrison
- *Entrepreneurial Strategic Management* by Ken R. Blawatt
- *Achieving Success in Nonprofit Organizations* by Timothy J. Kloppenborg
- *Leading Latino Talent to Champion Innovation* by Vinny Caraballo
- *Developing Successful Business Strategies: Gaining the Competitive Advantage* by Rob Reider
- *First and Fast: Outpace Your Competitors, Lead Your Markets, and Accelerate Growth* by Stuart Cross
- *Strategies for University Management* by J. Mark Munoz and Neal King
- *Strategies for University Management, Volume II* by J. Mark Munoz and Neal King
- *Strategic Organizational Alignment: Authority, Power, Results* by Chris Crosby
- *Business Strategy in the Artificial Intelligence Economy* by J. Mark Munoz and Al Naqvi
- *Strategic Engagement: Practical Tools to Raise Morale and Increase Results, Volume I: Core Activities* by Chris Crosby
- *Strategic Engagement: Practical Tools to Raise Morale and Increase Results, Volume II: System-Wide Activities* by Chris Crosby
- *How to Navigate Strategic Alliances and Joint Ventures: A Concise Guide For Managers* by Meeta Dasgupta

Announcing the Business Expert Press Digital Library

Concise e-books business students need for classroom and research

This book can also be purchased in an e-book collection by your library as

- a one-time purchase,
- that is owned forever,
- allows for simultaneous readers,
- has no restrictions on printing, and
- can be downloaded as PDFs from within the library community.

Our digital library collections are a great solution to beat the rising cost of textbooks. E-books can be loaded into their course management systems or onto students' e-book readers.

The **Business Expert Press** digital libraries are very affordable, with no obligation to buy in future years. For more information, please visit **www.businessexpertpress.com/librarians**. To set up a trial in the United States, please email **sales@businessexpertpress.com**.

9 781951 527761